T0280177

A Classic Adirondack Paddle

BOOKS
NORTH COUNTRY BOOKS

An imprint of Globe Pequot, the trade division of
The Rowman & Littlefield Publishing Group, Inc.
4501 Forbes Blvd., Ste. 200
Lanham, MD 20706
www.rowman.com

Distributed by NATIONAL BOOK NETWORK

British Library Cataloguing in Publication Information Available

Library of Congress Cataloging-in-Publication Data

ISBN 9781493078912 (cloth : alk. paper) | ISBN 9781493078899 (pbk. : alk. paper) |
ISBN 9781493078905 (electronic)

♾️™ The paper used in this publication meets the minimum requirements of American
National Standard for Information Sciences—Permanence of Paper for Printed Library
Materials, ANSI/NISO Z39.48-1992

A Classic Adirondack Paddle

*Including a Visit with Noah John Rondeau
the Hermit of Cold River Flow*

FUN AND ADVENTURE IN SCOUTING

William J. O'Hern

BOOKS
NORTH COUNTRY BOOKS

Essex, Connecticut

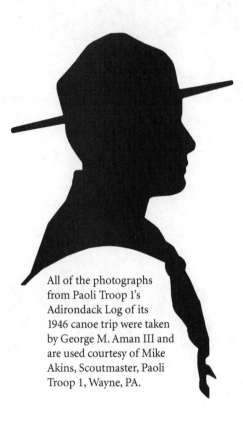

TABLE OF CONTENTS

ACKNOWLEDGEMENTS

For permission to reprint the ADIRONDACK LOG of Paoli Troop 1 Boy Scouts of America, June 15 to 30, 1946, created and compiled by George M. Aman III, William Z. McLear III, and Herbert J. Henderson, grateful acknowledgement is made to the creators and to Mike Akins, Scoutmaster of Paoli Troop 1, Wayne, PA.

Grateful acknowledgement is made to the late George Glyndon Cole, Editor and Publisher, of *North Country Life* for permission to reprint the Lucius Russell portion of William H. "Billy: Burger's "Some Conservation Men," original material that appeared in *North Country Life*, Summer 1950 and William H. Burger's "George Moran of Raquette Falls," original material that appeared in *North Country Life*, Spring 1952. Burger's article was later reprinted in *Adirondack Kaleidoscope* and *North Country Characters* (In the Adirondacks, May 2013), and appears here as "Raquette Falls, the Last Adirondack Frontier" with permission of In the Adirondacks.

For permission to reprint Clayt Seagears' "Hermit of Cold River" that appeared in *The New York State Conservationist* October–November 1946 issue, grateful acknowledgement is made to the author, to *The New York State Conservationist*, and to Eileen C. Stegemann, Assistant Editor of the *Conservationist* magazine.

Grateful acknowledgement is made to *The Northern Logger & Timber Processor* and Erin Kessler, Executive Editor where "Adirondack Logger Rescues an Iconic Hermit's Cabin," by William J. O'Hern first appeared in the November 2022 issue.

Cover image: "Long Lake, looking north from New York State Route 30, Hamilton County, in the Adirondack Mountains." Photograph by Marc Wanner, ©2023.

DEDICATION

To the creators of Adirondack Log of Paoli Troop 1
(left to right) Herbert J. "Hobey" Henderson,
William Z. "Bill" McLear III, and George M. Aman.

and

Richard A. "Dick" Henderson, shown with his wife,
Alisan in 2018 at their Wayne, PA, home of 60 years. Two years
following the Paoli Troop 1 1946 canoe expedition, Dick
found that interest and passion had motivated him and his brother
Hobey to join the Adirondack Mountain Club (ADK).
Dick treasures his Kodachrome slides snapped with his new Argus C3
camera during the summer of 1948 when
he worked as a hut boy at ADK's Johns Brook Lodge (JBL).

At 94, Dick continues to exhibit the same spirit
that served him so well as a first class scout. This project would
never have materialized without his leadership.

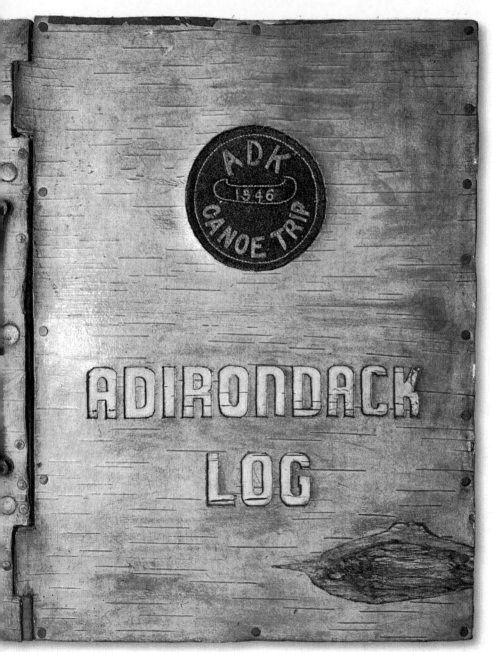

The cover of Paoli Troop 1's Special Book. Courtesy Mike Akins, Scoutmaster of Paoli Troop 1

A SPECIAL BOOK

Primary sources of information, such as scrapbooks, journals and diaries, letters and postcards, voice recordings and photo albums help one relate in a personal way to events of the past. They promote a deeper understanding of history as a series of human events which can be more deeply explored with every new piece of evidence.

The cover of the hermit's 1946 journal. Noah John Rondeau wrote his 1946 journal almost entirely in an enigmatic code that resembled the "footprints of an inebriated hen." Courtesy The Adirondack Experience at Blue Mountain Lake.

Aside from human memory and the unrecorded oral transmission of information from generation to generation, histories based on primary sources are really the only way the current generation can hope to relate to and understand what happened before.

That is the case with the discovery of this 1946 Boy Scout trip journal's survival. The Adirondack Log of Paoli Troop 1 is a true blessing to those who enjoy canoeing and hiking in the same area today. Readers can only imagine

	NO. OF MEALS	LIMIT	AMOUNT	Cost
FOOD BOX TO BE PACKED UP AT LONG LAKE POST OFFICE THURSDAY JUNE 20				
2nd package				
✓ BACON	5	5 lb CANS	1	
✓ JAM	8	6 oz CAN	32	•
✓ LEMONADE POWDER	1	PK	TO MAKE 2 GAL	
CHOCOLATE BARS ½ lb. BARS	6	BAR	24	
POTATOES, DEHYDRATED	2	4 lb PAIL	1	
TOMATOES, CANNED	1	CAN	2	
✓ COCOA	6	½ lb lbs	20 10	
✓ MUFFIN MIX (OR INGRED.)	5	PK	15	
✓ TUNA FISH (FOR BERGSON)	1	CAN	1	
✓ PRUNES	4	lbs	8	
✓ APRICOTS	2	lbs.	6	
✓ PEACHES	1	lbs.	3	
✓ APPLES, DRIED	1	lbs.	3	
✓ FIGS	1	lbs.	3	
EGGS, POWDERED	2 + BAKING	?	EQUIV. OF 3 DOZ	
✓ WHEATINA	1	BOX	1	
✓ CORN BREAD MIX (OR INGRED.)	2	PKS	6	
✓ SALT TABLETS	—		100	
✓ RICE	2	lbs.	4	
✓ DRIED PEAS	1	lbs	3	
✓ TEA	2	TEA BALLS	32	
✓ PREPARED PIE CRUST (OR INGRED.)	1	PK	3 PIES	
✓ SOUP, POWDERED CHICKEN	1	PK.	4	
✓ CAKE MIX (OR INGRED.)	1	PK.	3	

Dick Henderson commented, "I am quite intrigued by these [well organized in-advance of the expedition] pages of food supplies needed for the canoe trip! Although I am listed on the first few pages of the Adirondack Log as being Commissary Chief, I have remembered absolutely nothing about such a project, except…looking at these lists, I see a few handwritten words on them that look like mine. Old white-haired Miss Darlington at Radnor taught us penmanship in the style of the Declaration of Independence. And I see more of the words that look to be written in the style of my mother…." Courtesy Mike Akins, Scoutmaster of Paoli Troop 1

how much the boys in the journal—now elderly men—enjoy reliving the adventure that was carefully preserved in words and photographs by their fellow scouts and now will be further preserved for later generations in this small publication.

The discovery of this 75-year-old log makes it fun and interesting to learn about historical events in the words and images of the direct participants. Besides, everything worth discovering and learning about hasn't been written in a formal history text—not by a long shot.

Another editor and I have altered this text and captions very minimally, only for such purposes as to render it easier to read and to make spelling consistent. Throughout, our goal has been to preserve the original to the extent possible.

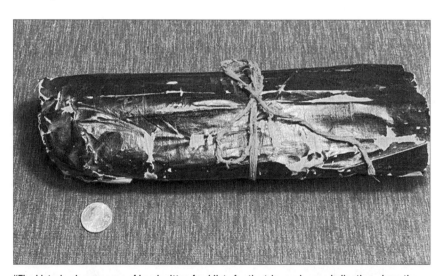

"The historic eleven pages of handwritten food lists for the trip, each page indicating where the food would be bought along the way, were contained in a black oil cloth container which went along with the scouts on the trip. My dad had the lists within the oil cloth for the last 75 years!" —**Chad Henderson**. Courtesy Chad Henderson

Paoli Troop 1's Adirondack log is written, I believe, on older paper made with high cotton fiber content. For its age, it is actually in better condition after being stored for seventy-five years than some newer primary sources I have seen printed on newer high-wood pulp paper. Nearly a century old, the paper is brittle and crumbles easily. The photographs are faded and some curled, but the images portray a marvelous canoe journey and that is a standard trip still taken today by all sorts of groups.

The contents are neatly organized with an introduction and a list of members and positions. There are maps that were used to guide the fleet of canoes, a listing of the daily menus, songs sung, souvenirs collected and autographs of some participants.

The fifty-plus-page text that tells the daily story is typed. Snapshots are carefully affixed and arranged tastefully to illustrate the sixteen-day unfolding tale.

Dick Henderson reported that Hobey Henderson and George Aman, "with authority…sat out on George's porch and composed the text of the Adirondack Log together. That makes sense because Hobey was the Master of sequence of events, and George was the Master of what event was happening when a photo was snapped." George reports Bill McLear's contribution to the Log has been lost in the passage of time.

This photo of the group of Pennsylvania Boy Scouts was found in Noah John Rondeau's photo album. He labeled it "Penn. Scouts." Courtesy Richard J. Smith from Rondeau's photo album

I am always excited to find such an interesting document that speaks of the mountains and waters "Up North." It is just the kind of jewel story-tellers seek, collect, and share. It's an open-ended quest I'll always do.

Reading the Adirondack Log was, I can only guess, as much fun for its makers as seeing memorable landscapes in print.

The hermit casting from one of his favorite perches. Rocky, boulder-strewn Cold River is a scenic paradise. Courtesy Jay L. Gregory

Being curious about the log's whereabouts, I asked participant Richard "Dick" Henderson about the priceless journal that had a long shelf life. Where had the document been all these long years? Judging from the yellowing of paper and photos, I assumed it might have been exposed to light and maybe extremes of heat. Yet despite the cumulative, irreversible damage, the document was still an interesting portrait painted from a real-life experience.

The answer to my question came to Dick from his brother, Herb "Hobey" Henderson:

> George Aman and I wrote, typed and compiled the pages of the log at his house in Wayne, PA, later that notable summer of 1946. When I had the log bolted together using its wood cover (made by poor-carpenter me), I built a special cardboard box to protect the book that form-fit the log. It was then tucked away in my bottom bureau drawer awaiting further advice as to where it should be held in perpetuity.
>
> And our dear log stayed in that same bureau drawer for many, many years as I completed my education, served in the army, worked, and moved from hither to yon all over the USA

for many years. Finally, sometime before 2011, I rescued the book from its safe jail and gave it to Dick during one of our frequent trips to Pennsylvania and Maine, confident that he could find an appropriate home for it. Dick gave the log to co-author George Aman who I understand presented it to Paoli 1 at their 100th anniversary affair. Paoli 1 at that time had a safe place in which to keep it for the inspiration of future Boy Scouts.

BUT WAIT! THERE'S MORE! A new discovery! In that same bureau drawer has lain hidden all these years a very beat-up oil cloth packet containing hand-printed lists of food/provision items needed for the trip that were to be purchased in Wayne, PA, and along the trip at small Adirondack stores. A gem!"

So, there's the story of the log for you who have immersed yourselves in a magnificent historical project.

Cold River City. The Adirondack Mountains is a land of high rock-faced and forested summits and rolling hills, with more lakes and streams than can easily be counted. Courtesy Gay Prue

INTRODUCTION

A VACATION PARADISE

The Paoli 1 Boy Scouts' trip took place in America's rarest playground—the ancient Adirondack Mountains—which has been known as "A Vacation Paradise" for more than a century. Nearly four million acres in extent in 1946 when the outing that is chronicled in the following pages took place, this vast playground embraces more than 1,500 lakes of all sizes and depths and at varying altitudes, comparable in splendor and picturesqueness with the famous lakes of the world. Nearly 2,000 mountains, many of them forest-clad, some with rock-faced peaks towering into the air for more than 5,000 feet, add their majestic grandeur to the natural panorama. Here the moods of nature inspire the spirit of freedom and play. Here city life is forgotten, business and social cares are cast aside, and concern gives way to the joy of living out-of-doors.

Several decades earlier, automobiling in and about this famous resort region was made possible by the perfected system of state highways. The development of accommodations at hotels, boarding houses, state-run campgrounds, boat launches, and lean-tos made the vast area "A Vacation Paradise" for thousands of tourists and vacationists who now had access to the woods and waters and could choose lodging that varied from primitive to luxurious. The recreational possibilities afforded in this vast state playground were so diversified in character that unlimited opportunities were offered for every kind of outdoor sport.

This was what the group of teenage Pennsylvania Boy Scouts found in June 1946 when they came to launch a small fleet of rented canoes or an extended vacation that offered natural beauty, history and a special Adirondack character they would long remember.

Their route took them on what is today the Adirondack Ninety-mile Canoe Classic from Old Forge to Saranac Lake. This is also the first section of today's Northern Forest Canoe Trail, considered the waterway equivalent of the Appalachian Trail, which extends via rivers, streams, lakes, and carries to Fort Kent, Maine.

In 1946 World War II had ended, the United Nations International Children's Emergency Fund (UNICEF) was established, War Crimes Tribunals

The Adirondacks is a diverse country of dense un-lumbered tracts, broken by bogs and swamps where tangling alders and the black spruce grow. Courtesy Leigh Portner

were held in Nuremberg and Tokyo, bikinis went on sale in Paris, and by June Boy Scouts of Paoli Troop 1 in Wayne, Pennsylvania, were planning an Adirondack canoe expedition. The troop's scribes, George Aman, Bill McLear, and Herb Henderson, who documented the scouts' preparations and journey, reported on scoutmaster William Patterson's canoe proposal:

"When the itinerary was made public the boys' interest reached a high level and the preparations began at once. During early June many short meetings were held each week at the home of William Patterson. Many boys began purchasing equipment and supplies. Menus were made and then the gigantic job of food buying was started. Meanwhile such jobs as contracting for canoe rental, obtaining maps, and many other details were handled by Bill Patterson. Money and applications were collected by Ted Kennedy.

Flat tires were common on early Adirondack road trips. Courtesy Leigh Portner

"Finally, a last-minute meeting was held at Mr. Krick's house, where equipment was checked and weighed in. At last it seemed that the trip was a reality."

Dick Henderson told me Herb "Hobey" Henderson, his older brother, served as the trip scribe, while Bill McLear held the important post of trip first-aid, and George Aman was the trip photographer. Dick said "All are alive and well" in October 2021.

Dick, 92 in 2021, has an apt way of saying what it means to have spent a stirring canoe expedition 75 summers ago over a 125-mile-chain-of-lakes paddle from Old Forge to Saranac Lake in the Adirondack Mountains right after the end of World War II.

Plumley's Landing, Long Lake, Circa 1945. There are stands of virgin timber, white pine, big hemlocks, and dwarf spruce on mountainsides with gnarled branches that point eastward—the direction the prevailing wind blows. Courtesy Albert "Bud" Smith

"The highlight of the trip," he says, "was a detour to visit the hermit of the Adirondacks, Noah John Rondeau. His camp on the Cold River is a very inaccessible location for most people to reach. It's because Noah John kept journals and recorded our coming that Paoli Troop 1 became a part of the lore of the Adirondacks."

Dick emailed me a favorite snapshot as he pointed out, "I'm the scout leaning over Noah John's shoulder. He must have turned occasionally to speak directly to me, because I've always carried a memory of a one-to-one talk with the hermit."

Dick was one of fifteen Boy Scouts who were led on their paddling adventure by scoutmaster William C. Patterson and Colonel Clifton Lisle. He spearheaded the search for the whereabouts of the scouts' decades-old log that surfaced in October 2021 in the Paoli scouts' archive. The birch bark cover, designed by Herbert J. Henderson, is titled

ADIRONDACK LOG
of
Paoli Troop 1
BSA
June 15 to 30, 1946

It reads "Compiled by George M. Aman 3rd, William Z. McLear 3rd, and Herbert J. Henderson." The compilers dedicated the photo journal to "the future Scouts who may read this book."

Page three of the scrapbook lists the participants and their duties. It reads:

MEMBERS AND	POSITIONS
Colonel Clifton Lisle	
William C. Patterson	Leader
George M. Aman 3rd	Photographer
David Aronson	Navigator
Niles Beeson	Assistant Quartermaster
Jeff Aronson	Absolutely Nothing
John Clutz	Assistant Canoe Repair
Herbert J. Henderson	Scribe
Richard A. Henderson	Commissary Chief
John Holtzapple	Mail Orderly (Male Disorderly)
Stuart Horton	Assistant Commissary
Robert T. Ives	Assistant First Aid
Edgar S. Kennedy JR.!!	Finances
Donald I. Lamont	Quartermaster and Bugler
William Z. McLear	First Aid
Peter Schultz	Fire Warden
Paul Clark	Assistant leader and canoe repair

What follows, in pictures taken by George M. Aman and text from the scouts' Adirondack log book, are the events that portray the canoers' arrival at Old Forge on Saturday, June 15, 1946, and conclusion with the end of their Adirondack classic canoe journey at Saranac Lake Village.

Cold River Lean-to 4, 1946. Thousands of square miles are covered with green canopy which attracts a wide variety of people. And everywhere you go there are plenty of spruce and balsam, the trees that provide the forest scent, the healthy potpourri that does strange things to one's mind. Courtesy Albert "Bud" Smith

George Aman. Troop 1 photographer had much to aim his camera's lens at. Courtesy Mike Akin, Scoutmaster of Troop 1

Noah John Rondeau, hermit of Cold River Flow, was the highlight of the trip. Courtesy C.V. Latimer Jr., M.D.

Dick Henderson is the scout leaning over the hermit's shoulder. Dick said, "I'm sure Noah spoke directly to me, but I don't remember." Courtesy Richard J. Smith. Photo found in the Hermit's collection

Eagle scout Phillip G. Wolff, Circa 1936. Over the years, the hermitage had been a popular destination for many scouts. At 94-years old (in 2010), Wolff shared his pictures and his day-long visit with the hermit with me. His story, "Nothing Beat Cold River," appeared in *The Hermit and Us: Our Adventures with Noah John Rondeau* by William J. O'Hern (In the Adirondacks, 2014). In the early 1930s Wolff spent summers living with his aunt and uncle in Saranac Lake. His camping partner was Frosty Bradley. Wolff shared, "As two Eagle scouts in our early 20s, hiking, mountain climbing, and canoeing were good excuses to go camping. We prided ourselves on living and eating in the woods with the lightest possible loads." Courtesy Phillip G. Wolff

Backpacking gear was much simpler in the 1930s. Courtesy Phillip G. Wolff

"Rondeau territory." Wolff's first glimpse of the hermitage. Wolff's and Bradley's first Duck Hole campsite several miles above Big Dam. Wolff said, "Ranger Searles suggested that one of our first projects should be a visit to the hermit." Courtesy Phillip G. Wolff

Cold River City, 1936. "We arrived at the Town Hall one morning and were greeted by Noah, who was in his 50s, with a hearty hello and a handshake," said Wolff. "We were surprised at his short stature. We had been told Noah's two weaknesses were smoking and reading, so we brought two packs of pipe tobacco and some magazines." The hermit's huts were constructed from salvaged materials. Courtesy Phillip G. Wolff

Big Dam, built by the Santa Clara Lumber Company, once impounded a huge reservoir known as Cold River Flow. It was the backbone that allowed logs to be flushed downstream to Raquette River. Vague evidence today remains of the once substantial dam that spanned Cold River. Courtesy Phillip G. Wolff

Wolff said he took this snapshot of a pair of handmade leather mittens Rondeau was curing.
Courtesy Phillip G. Wolff

"Noah was fairly good with his homemade bow and arrows," recalled Wolff. "Noah said he had neither a fishing nor hunting license. He also had various systems set up around camp and area trails to check if a stranger was in 'his township.'" Courtesy Phillip G. Wolff

Noah posed puffing his "goose egg" meerschaum pipe. Wolff said, "Although religion was also off-limits, he felt the Ten Commandments were 'just common sense' and 'made civilization possible.' He also believed in a form of evolution and the existence of a supreme being, which, he said 'you could call God if you wished.'" Courtesy Phillip G. Wolff

Wolff snapped this view of Cold River below Duck Hole dam spillway. Phil Wolff said he never forgot Noah John's hospitality. "Rondeau chose an entirely different path in life, but that doesn't mean he turned out wrong. People are like varieties of mountain flora and fauna. Some survive well in a domestic setting, being cared for and sheltered, while some need to live wild and roam free. Noah John recognized what was in his nature and accepted it." Courtesy Phillip G. Wolff

Chapter 1

WE'RE OFF

MINUTES AND PICTURES
Saturday, June 15, 1946

At five-thirty on Saturday morning the members of the expedition met at Mr. Krick's house and when all the cars had arrived the loading began. At five forty-five the first car departed. At six o'clock Bill Patterson called to remind Mrs. Aronson that her sons Jeff and Tinker were a half hour overdue. In fifteen minutes they arrived and the last car left shortly afterwards. The only accident to break the monotony of the ten-and-a-half-hour journey was a tire blowout on Mr. Krick's car. The Henderson car stopped to purchase fresh food at Utica, N.Y. and consequently arrived at Old Forge last.

Breakfast is being served on Sunday. Notice the square eating pans.

Here the boys are hungrily devouring their breakfast.

As the boys stepped from their respective cars they were met by a swarm of unfriendly insects but soon the cars were unloaded and a temporary camp was established by the First Lake of the Fulton Chain near the Rivett Boat Livery. While supper was being cooked a meeting of the staff was held and numbers were given to each boy. Numbers one to five were given the

Packed and ready to leave, the boys happily formed for this picture. Notice the fresh civilized-looking faces.

detail known as "wood and water," six to ten took "cooking" and eleven to fifteen had "cleanup." The details were to rotate each day. After a good supper the members were allowed to go into the town where they bought such articles as insect repellent and mosquito netting. Upon returning to camp most of the members retired but Paul Clark and Niles Beeson went on a frog hunt.

The canoes are lined up by the shore at First Lake lean-to, where the party ate lunch on Sunday.

Here the boys are preparing lunch at First Lake lean-to.

Sunday, June 16: Reveille was blown at six o'clock on this cold and misty morning. After a short delay breakfast was cooked and eaten. Then while several went to church the remainder began packing the equipment on the new pack frames. After much difficulty resulting in a not-too-expert packing, the packs were transferred a short distance to the dock of Rivett's Boat Livery. There when accounts had been settled with Mr. Rivett the canoes were loaded and the party departed.

After paddling for three miles, they came to the lean-to at the far shore of First Lake. When lunch was being prepared it was discovered that a watermelon for lunch had been left behind. Three boys volunteered to go back for it and after being absent for two hours they returned with the prize. Lunch was soon completed and the canoes shoved off for the Third Lake lean-to where they were to spend the night. As soon as this place was reached the canoes were unloaded and the boys went for a swim. Dinner was served a bit late that night but everyone enjoyed it and showed their approval in a song fest that followed. Near the end of the evening Colonel Lisle gave a talk to the boys in which he praised their start and recommended some improvements. He also discussed the Scout Oath and Law. Then the boys retired to their newly built canoe shelters.

The canoeists ate their first dinner in the wilds with much relish and a grain of salt.

Third Lake lean-to the morning after.

The boys marched into the town of Inlet, where they purchased more new insect repellant.

Here the boys are reading some comic books they bought in the town of Inlet.

The troop ate lunch on Monday on the bank of a highway between Fifth and Sixth Lakes. The classic expressions on their face are not accountable.

Chapter 2

CARRY TO SIXTH LAKE

Monday, June 17: The troop arose at six-thirty and rapidly jumped into their clothes to escape the swarms of insects that had bothered them all night. As breakfast was being prepared letters to families and others were written by many of the boys. A lack of pure water necessitated the use of lake water and halazone tablets.

By ten, the canoes were packed and the party departed. The narrow inlet into Fourth Lake was traversed and then Fourth Lake itself was crossed. After moments of indecision the inlet into Fifth Lake was found. The canoes were on the shore of Fifth Lake by the highway and the boys marched to the nearby town of Inlet. After purchasing supplies and mailing letters the

Niles Beeson and Herbert Henderson strain beneath the unaccustomed weight of a canoe in one of the earlier carries.

party returned to the canoes and ate lunch. The lunch was topped off by some ice cream purchased for the boys by Colonel Lisle. The cleanup detail removed refuse of the meal while the boys began preparing for their first

John Clutz, fondly referred to as "broadbottom" for obvious reasons, is shown here carrying a canoe on a portage.

portage. The portage into Sixth Lake was very short and was completed successfully after a rather long time.

After disembarking, several of the boys noticed storm clouds on the horizon which increased as the canoes proceeded across Sixth and Seventh Lakes. The weather became very threatening and rain fell as the party discovered the lean-to on Seventh Lake. The canoes were quickly unloaded and everything put in the shelter of the lean-to. Then the rain suddenly stopped and the boys went swimming. Refreshed by their swim and encouraged by the stopping of the rain, all pitched in and made a camp and started supper. Another reason for the sudden completion of the swim was the approach of a strange canoe which was believed to contain some women campers.

Dick Henderson, one of the "dampened spirits," drying his sleeping bag under the canopy at Seventh Lake lean-to.

An especially good dinner was then eaten, during which a light rain began to fall. While the cleanup detail was doing its work, Niles Beeson, Dick Henderson, and John Clutz ventured into the water again. Herbert Henderson and Bill Patterson who were suffering from sore ears and Colonel Lisle who had a thorn in his finger soaked these parts in hot water and boric acid.

Soon everyone was preparing for bed and at 10:00 Taps was blown. Much to the discomfort of those sleeping outside the lean-to, new lakes were formed under their sleeping bags by the rain which began to fall shortly after taps.

Colonel Lisle with full pack, a paddle, and the first aid kit which he carried through one of the portages. The curious cloth around his neck is a piece of cheesecloth used for mosquito netting.

Chapter 3

RAQUETTE LAKE BOUND

Tuesday, June 18: This morning the campers were awakened by the unhappy sight of rain. Those who were in the shelter suffered little but those in the tents and canoe shelters were mostly soaked. The rain continued but the prospect of a good breakfast soon cooking cheered dampened spirits. After breakfast a canopy was erected in front of the lean-to under which the wet sleeping bags and tents were dried. Soon the rain stopped and by 10:45 the packs were packed. The packs were soon ferried to the first portage a quarter of a mile away.

The portage into Eighth Lake was a mile long and was accomplished under clearing skies. Several of the boys who were tired of halazone water filled their canteens at a pump found near the middle of the portage.

A stiff wind was felt coming over the lake at the end of the carry. As the canoes were being packed, Bill Patterson doled out the customary portage chocolate. Because of the wind and high waves, the canoes were forced to stay near the north shore.

After paddling an hour across Eighth Lake, the beginning of the next portage was found. This portage, terminating at Brown's Tract Inlet, was longer than expected. Trouble was encountered at trail intersections and boys carrying canoes were forced to backtrack several times.

After completing the carry, they began the long paddle down the inlet. This inlet turned out to be nothing more than a winding swamp stream. Finally, crossing under a road bridge the canoeists sighted Raquette Village close by on Raquette Lake. The time for lunch had long since passed due to mishaps, but no lunch had been eaten as yet.

Decking the canoes, the boys trouped into the Raquette Lake Supply Co. general store. Here food was purchased and because of the late hour a brief lunch was eaten at the ice cream counter. At the post office mail and parcels of food were gotten. The members hurried back to the canoes and "weighed anchor" to find their night's shelter.

Soon a large island was sighted having the appropriate name of Big Island. On this island the boys found the first completely bug-free campsite of the journey. The canoes were quickly unloaded and because of the late hour dinner and camp pitching were started at once. The boys were so happy to be free of the bugs even for a time that they undertook such vigorous enterprises as chopping down a fair-sized tree (completed with many cries of "Timberrr") and the washing of some dirty clothes. After such labors the steak dinner served by the cooks was welcomed heartily and eaten without a moment's delay.

After supper Niles Beeson, Herbert Henderson and George Aman undertook a very short swim although the air was rather chilly and the water even colder. Later on in the evening hot soup which had been purchased in Raquette Village was served to the boys as a "night cap." After this bit of refreshment, they turned in to sleep soundly without the usual bug ridden dreams.

Eighth Lake from the end of the first portage. Notice the rough water beginning to "kick up."

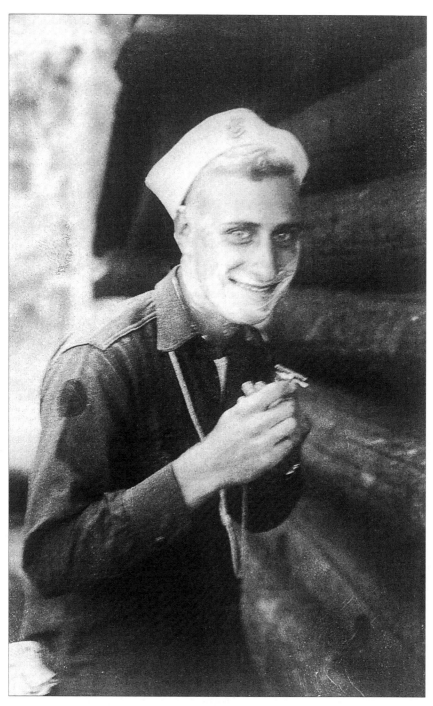

It was a "close shave" for the photographer who finally succeeded in getting this record shot of "Boots" Clark performing one of his rare razor feats.

The expressions on these faces testify as to the length of the portage into Brown's Tract Inlet, which they are just finishing.

Standing in front of the general store at Raquette Village are H. Henderson and Bill McLear. The heavy clothing was worn because of the windy weather.

Chapter 4

ONWARD TO FORKED LAKE

Wednesday, June 19: A fire was started very early on this morning for the very important use of warming cold boys. A heavy dew had fallen during the night and so after a good breakfast clothes, tents and ponchos which had been exposed to the night air were dried in the sun.

At ten-thirty the canoes set out across Raquette Lake. After a journey of more than an hour the canoes came to the portage into Forked Lake. Here the party met up with some lady campers who were on the same itinerary as the Scouts. While preparing to portage they discovered that a water can had been left behind at Big Island.

The party eating supper at Big Island lean-to. The man at the far left is Mr. Marvin, a camper who was our guest at dinner.

Here the boys are industriously writing letters to families and other friends.

At the end of the portage, time out was taken as the cooks prepared lunch. The boys then packed the canoes and started off across the lake. After crossing Forked Lake in good time the party prepared to make the day's second portage across falls in the Raquette River. These were at the outlet of Forked Lake. Several boys went to see the falls or rapids as they turned out to be.

The clothes and other articles drying on a point at Big Island. Some of these articles were washed, others had been wetted by the dew.

Soon packed and canoes were shouldered and the hard 1½ mile portage over a poor trail was begun. At the end of the carry the boys found the lean-to where they were to spend the night. Almost upon their arrival swarms of bloodthirsty black flies greeted the party, whereupon all sought safety in mosquito netting.

The boys took a little while to prepare for the portage to Forked Lake. Perhaps the attractive women campers resting in the immediate vicinity were connected with this delay.

Here "Tinker" Aronson is helping a canoe carrier to withstand the gusts of wind at the end of a portage.

This picture was taken as Bill Patterson came staggering in to the terminal end of the Forked Lake carry. He was last to come through—those women again! (*See top caption, previous page.*)

At a pier near the end of the portage into Forked Lake, the party ate lunch.

The wood and water detail made a fire in the fireplace and they went out and got wood for the first baking fire of the trip. Then the cooks were taught the lore of baking by Bill Patterson. Several canoe shelters were erected. Finally, dinner including the corn bread baked under the direction of Hobey Henderson was prepared and eaten amid many favorable remarks. As the clean-up detail did their work after supper, more muffins were baked for breakfast.

When an hour had passed several boys enjoyed a brisk bath by sitting in the rapids of the river. The one accident of the trip occurred when Niles Beeson cut his foot on a can while swimming. However, he was expertly treated by Bill McLear while the onlookers contributed such remarks as "Amputate at the neck!" The swimmers warmed themselves by the fire and then went to bed.

The party canoes down the Raquette River shortly after completing a portage on Thursday.

At Raquette River camp the boys did their first baking in the new reflector ovens. "Boots" Clark is trying to avoid the smoke.

One of the better cooks of the trip specializing in original dishes, Jeff Aronson is here undoubtedly concocting some new creation at the camp on the Raquette River on Wednesday.

Chapter 5

LONG LAKE

Thursday, June 20: The boys were awakened by reveille at 6:30 on this bright but chilly morning. A fire was quickly started and the boys not working on preparing breakfast began dismantling shelters. The muffins baked the night before were eaten with relish and large amounts of jelly. By devious methods it was discovered that today was the birthday of John Clutz, alias "J.C." alias "Broadbottom." After breakfast the duffels were packed on the frames and the party paddled downstream to the first short portage. After completing this portage, the canoes traversed a short distance and then came into the inlet of Long Lake. After going partway down the lake, they came to the village of Long Lake. Here, after beaching canoes, the boys went into the

Long Lake village where the boys stopped on Thursday, June 20. Here Colonel Lisle left the party.

The rocky shore at the Catlin Bay shelter on Long Lake.

town and while supplies were bought, ate huge quantities of ice cream. Also, a new paddle was purchased to replace a broken one. The boys also inquired about the Louis-Conn fight which they found out had been won by Louis. All were sorry to bid Colonel Lisle farewell. He had to return home because of business. Mail was inquired for, but since it would not yet be in for two

Here the canoers are dodging boulders near one end of Long Lake. In the foreground are Dan Lament and Ted Kennedy.

This is a picture of Long Lake from the lower end. It was taken from a canoe.

hours it was decided to leave the mail orderly behind for it. While eating a light lunch on the beach, several boys noticed an overcast forming on the horizon. The clouds became thicker and the water became rough as the party searched for Catlin Bay, which was their destination for the night. They discovered one camp, but believing it to be the wrong one, they moved on. When they had worked their way off the navigator's map, they decided to return but found the right camp finally with the help of the mail orderly who was met. Rain began to fall as camp was pitched. Again, a canopy was erected as everyone prepared for a storm. Tents and canoe shelters were hastily made and then supper was begun. The rain multiplied the difficulties of pitching camp, so dinner was very late. After dinner the rain slackened a bit but it was very late and by the time a sketchy job of clean-up had been done it was time for the exhausted boys to retire. After a bit of talking the boys heard the faint notes of taps and sleep came while the rain continued.

Friday, June 21: The previous night Bill Patterson had said that the boys could sleep late in the morning and his wishes were carried out to the fullest. After a hearty breakfast and lunch combined, at eleven o'clock the boys started breaking camp. Realizing that the regular destination could not be reached, no one hurried. After transporting the packs to the shore, the party loaded up and departed about one o'clock. Instead of the regular destination of Seward lean-to, the party only went a short way down the Raquette River after traversing the rest of Long Lake. The water on Long Lake was very rough.

Calkins Creek lean-to was where the party spent the night on Friday. This creek enters [the Cold River which flows into the] Raquette River below Long Lake.

On closer inspection Calkins Creek lean-to is seen to be a rather nice one. The tent is being erected by "Boots" Clark.

Supper is in the making at Calkins Creek lean-to. The cooks are Dick Henderson and Bob Ives.

In the morning camp looked like this. The person sitting in the lean-to has mosquito netting on to escape the bugs.

This is another view of Calkins Creek lean-to from back in the woods. The camp is on a low hill by the bank of the creek.

Here is a view of the joining of Calkins Creek to the Cold River taken from the lean-to.

The boys cached the canoes a short way up the Cold River.

The party turned off the Raquette River into a tributary, the Cold River. A short way up the Cold River at the branching of Calkins Creek they found the lean-to. Here the canoes were unloaded and the packs carried up the steep incline to the shelter. Here was found an ample campsite including many mosquitoes. Supper was started almost immediately. The food was arranged in parcels for the caching of unnecessary articles with the canoes on the next day. After dinner a few hardy people went swimming and later on a short confab of all the members was held. Taps was blown at 10:45.

This is another picture of the process of caching canoes. Again, notice the mosquito netting.

Saturday, June 22: Boots Clark and Bill McLear got up early and started a fire and then went in swimming. The night was very buggy so the rest of the boys were soon up. Breakfast was begun, and equipment which would not be used in the hiking tour was wrapped in a poncho. After breakfast the lightened loads were lashed to the pack boards and the canoes were loaded. At 8:30 they weighed anchor and traveled up the Cold River until it became impassible. The canoes were beached and the canoes and articles to be cached were dragged into the woods.

After camouflaging the canoes and hanging the food bundles from ropes to protect them from porcupines, the hikers shouldered their loads and departed to find the trail to Shattuck Clearing. After a long, hard hike with much "bush-whacking" and walking through swamps, they reached the ranger station at the clearing. Lunch was then prepared. After a short rest the boys pushed on over the Northville-Placid Trail, which was found to be almost as rough as the old deer trails traversed during the morning. Two cable suspension bridges over the Moose Creek were crossed and then the rough hiking began. The boys had laughed at the simplicity of only a three-mile hike, but they soon found that hiking with 45-pound packs over rough terrain with the increasing number of bugs was not at all like a mere Saturday hike to Valley Forge. After walking through mud and climbing steep hills for an interminable time, they thought they had gone at least five or six miles. At one point they found a bubbling spring and took one of their many rests there.

Just when it seemed that the elusive Seward lean-to would never be sighted, they came down a long hill and saw by the trail one of the green shacks which was to be found near every lean-to. The weather had appeared threatening all day and now a few drops of rain fell, but although a canopy was erected the rain soon ceased and the skies cleared. The bugs in this wild region had become much worse, including a new variety of almost microscopic bug called midges which went right through mosquito netting and made everyone itch terribly.

Soon a supper was cooking, which took the novel form of Spam stew. It was cooked under the direction of Jeff Aronson, the cook with original ideas. After the stew had been eaten along with the usual baked muffins, (for five days while in the wilderness no fresh bread was available so all muffins etc. were made in reflector ovens), the boys were invited to partake of another original concoction made by Jeff. This dish, not so tempting perhaps, but thoroughly enjoyed, was afterwards known as chocolate oatmeal. It started life as chocolate pudding made with cocoa and oatmeal instead of corn starch. However, since it failed to thicken a quantity of flour and water paste was added. It was rather tasty but hit the bottoms of campers' stomachs like a rock, sometimes going right on through.

The evening was not without mishap, for in trying to clean his canteen cup Bob Ives slipped off a boulder and fell into the water of the aptly named Cold River. Later all went for a short swim in the shallow river. The water was very cold. By nine o'clock everyone was in bed.

A rear-view picture shows the column proceeding on the march and also shows the loads carried. The person in the lead, Jeff Aronson, is trail breaker and hence carries no pack.

The party ate lunch at the Shattuck Clearing Ranger Station on their way to Seward lean-to. The rangers were not home however.

Chapter 6

PAOLI TROOP 1 VISITS THE HERMIT OF COLD RIVER FLOW

Richard A. "Dick" Henderson of Wayne, PA, took me on a memory hike to see the Cold River hermit on June 23, 1946. It was quite a trip.

Dick was 92 years old in 2021. Seventy-five years ago, when he was a teenager, his Boy Scouts of America's Paoli, PA, Troop 1 beached their canoes at Pine Point, a mile above where Cold River empties into Long Lake, and

Alisan and Dick Henderson at the base of Big Slide Mountain. Left to Right: Upper Wolf Jaw, Armstrong, and Gothic Mountains, circa 1970. The lure of the woods, mountains, and water has been with Dick since his early scouting days along the path to self-reliance, citizenship, and physical fitness—along the trail to Eagle rank. Courtesy Richard A. Henderson.

The Seward Range seen from an opening on Cold River bluff. Author's photo

began a twelve-mile trek upriver to seek out Noah John Rondeau's lonely camp high up between the Seward and Santanoni mountain ranges.

Rondeau's camp was situated at an elevation of 1,950 feet and was flanked by seven peaks which top 4,000 feet. Paoli Troop 1 learned that at that altitude the growing season is short, and the hermit was not too optimistic about the prospects for the tiny garden which supplied him with most of his fresh vegetables.

Dick and I connected when he happened to read Rondeau's diary entry for June 23, 1946. The hermit wrote of that Sunday: "Nicest June day. 16 men and boys come, go (scouts)."

Dick, a retired engineer, had been reading my *Noah John Rondeau's Adirondack Wilderness Days* (The Forager Press, LLC, 2009) when he realized June 23 was the day he had been to the mountains to see where the famed Cold River hermit had settled two decades earlier.

The 1946 diary is written entirely in an elaborate cryptic-looking code—hermit hieroglyphics. Rondeau joked the coded journal was his "Fancy Diary" developed over years, and that it was filled with "Cob-web, Fly-Specks and wigwam smoke."

Although the hermit believed his enigmatic private code would never be broken, David Greene deciphered the code in the early 1990s and shared the

"The canoe trip started in black fly season. Many of the photos show our heads swathed in white netting. We dressed in traditional Army/Boy Scout shirts. White sailor caps were an old tradition. A number of us are seen wearing scratchy wool. I shudder a bit to think of it."—Dick Henderson.

contents of the mysterious journal with me. I turned the coded diary into a history book. *Noah John Rondeau's Adirondack Wilderness Days* shares those secret thoughts recorded in code.

Dick found Rondeau's translated diary fascinating. He learned that several days earlier, before his troop's arrival, the hermit had observed the "First Robin

Plantain bloom" and he cremated "Quilly in the Town Hall." Although there was a stretch of ideal June weather his "Potatoes and Nasturtiums froze" during the night of June 19.

Rondeau was known to point out to mountain climbers the direction old logging roads ran straight among the lines of trees. He told them how the wildflowers and wild game coexisted with his crops of vegetables, how straight and tall some of those early spruces grew.

As Dick and I emailed, we talked about the Adirondacks and what a conservationist is—someone who believes in the wise use of natural resources. I've never heard Noah John called an environmentalist. That's a fashionable, misused word.

Based on Rondeau's writings, I envision him as an independent Frenchman who wanted to live without evangelism and bureaucratic government decrees touching his life and that he cared very much about the flora and fauna that surrounded his wild-like life.

Standing, Left to Right: Herbert J. "Hobey" Henderson; William Z. "Bill" McLear; Richard A. "Dick" Henderson; Robert T. "Bob" Ives; John "Jack" Holtzapple; David Aronson; Edgar S. "Ted" Kennedy Jr.; John Clutz; John Aronson (behind J. Clutz), Peter Schultz; and Donald I. Lamont. Sitting, Left to Right: Niles Beeson; Paul "Boots" Clark; Stuart Horton; Noah John Rondeau; William C. "Bill" Patterson, Scoutmaster; and taking this photograph, Scout and Trip Photographer George M. Aman III.

The man knew the woods. Rondeau was like a topographic map that talked and told stories about ponds, and the maze of the lanes and forks in old corduroy logging roads that wound through the mountains, former lumber camps and landings where the lumbermen piled their logs.

Dick could take me back to those early Cold River days when the hermit's camp sat atop a bluff that overlooked deteriorating Big Dam, an old logging dam that once impounded millions of gallons of water that created Cold River Flow.

I looked forward to learning about Dick's meeting especially because he saw Rondeau in his native environment and could talk about several snapshots that were taken in camp that would add to the hermit's Adirondack folk-culture.

Dick Henderson's story begins.

The idea of taking the 1946 Adirondack Canoe Trip during black fly season almost surely came from Scoutmaster Bill Patterson. He had just come back from Europe at the end of World War II. I had been a Cub Scout coming up to 1941 and was trying to

Once the scouts reached Shattuck Clearing, they intersected the Northville-Placid Trail (N-P). The N-P Trail parallels Cold River, offering a multitude of scenic vistas. Courtesy Fred Studer

understand whether I could stand up to the rigors of becoming a Boy Scout, and Bill started to encourage me to join a WINTER troop venture to Boy Scout Camp Horseshoe, situated on the Mason-Dixon Line. I remember writing out a list of pros and cons, and finally going with the pros. It was an unusually snowy and cold winter. Inside the old wooden building that was our home, everything including the eggs froze. Outside, Bill encouraged me by showing me just how to split firewood. And I came to love it.

Rondeau was an inviting host. At first parties were required to identify themselves and certify their presence by signing a bound roster. Following a charade of formalities, a guided tour was offered. His two huts had signs designating the structures. Posted on the door of the Town Hall was a written list of gripes against the New York Conservation Department. In addition, the many tepees had given names. Courtesy Edward J. Fox

Our traditional Old Forge to Saranac Lake canoe trip, with a side trip to Cold River, would have required much planning—auto transportation, canoe rentals (definitely at Rivett's in Old Forge), food and hardware pick-up locations, and mail. And there must have been some way to reserve campsites for each night after a day's canoeing. Scout parents would have joined with trip leaders in carrying out the plans. And that daily need for having a secure location for the canoes at night would explain our necessarily short stay with Noah John. I remember well the "caching" of the canoes off in the woods beside the Cold River,

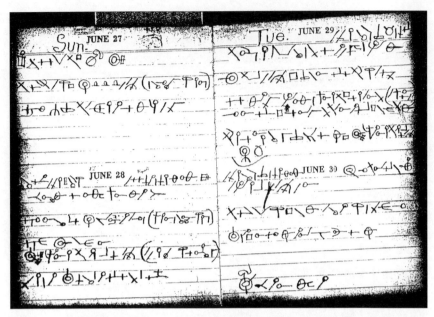

The hermit's mysterious coded hieroglyphics. Why would anyone spend so much time writing something no one else could decipher unless it was to describe the location of a hidden treasure? To that question, Rondeau was known to reply, "It's so no one else can read it." Evidently, he did not think it an onerous and senseless way of keeping things to himself. Maybe they were not worth reading. On the other hand, maybe they were directions to cached traps and overnight camps, great fishing holes, set locations for taking fur bearers or special deer hunting watches. Maybe, it was just a game he was playing with people so they could always have something to talk about. Author's photo

followed by the not-too-long hike into Noah John's camp. After the visit, we had to get back to the canoes, paddle back down the Cold River to Long Lake, and then on to the next campsite.

I remember that of course Noah John led us on an explanatory tour of his city. I was not only fascinated by this unusual man, but awed by his towering tepees made from long wooden poles—next winter's firewood. But I think the words we all remembered the most and that caused the most chuckles years later were at the end of an increasingly solemn prophecy: "and so a ring around the moon is a sign that the moon is in a ring."

George Aman had just turned seventeen shortly before the troop visited the hermitage. Perhaps because he was slightly older than the rest of the boys, scout leader Patterson gave him a Kodak Brownie camera and designated him as the group's photographer.

One snapshot shows the boys peering into the floorless, low-ceilinged huts. On the shelves were two-quart glass jars, filled with kitchen matches, flour, sugar, and salt. There were cans of baking soda and powder, some strange-looking cloth bags of synthetic butter, and powdered milk, old files, rope, and sawblades, pots and pans and other miscellaneous things.

The tepees held by far the greater attraction to Aman. The long poles with the log chains holding them together at the top, the big cast iron kettle suspended at the end of one chain over a fire, the ring of fireplace stones all presented themselves as subjects for the photographer. The hermit even struck a pose for George, demonstrating how he chopped notches in the logs.

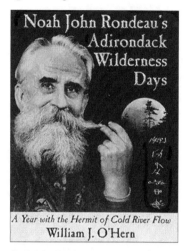

Noah John Rondeau's Adirondack Wilderness Days
A Year with the Hermit of Cold River Flow
William J. O'Hern

Noah John Rondeau's Adirondack Wilderness Days chronicles a year in the life of the hermit. Dick Henderson wrote the author after reading this book. Courtesy The Forager Press

And because of the lads' interest, Noah John shared how important the pole tepees were to his survival. The past winter had generally been regarded as unusually severe. His records showed he kept a wood fire burning in the oil drum stove continuously for 138 days without relighting it. Fortunately, except for the work of gathering and cutting poles, fuel was no problem in the Cold River country.

Dick added, "As to my recollection of things pertaining to Noah John personally, the memories are pretty thin because of the great length of time back. He was a huge presence, but I didn't find him in the least shocking, not in his clothes, his dwelling, his person. He was a warm, caring, amusing grandfather.

"I keep thinking that Bill Patterson could have alerted him in advance of the date of our arrival. Look at our group photograph. Noah and Bill seem to be in friendly, animated conversation. I imagine that just at that moment, Bill is promising Noah that he will send Noah copies of the pictures that were being taken."

Dick never mentioned if his fellow troop members considered Noah a hermit, a runaway recluse, or a romantic idealist, but there was no discussion of eccentricity, or of nonconformists who wanted to absent themselves from society, or whether he was a real hermit or not.

Rondeau's journal tells that deer had been more scarce the previous two falls than at any time in the 30 years he had been tramping the woods in what was probably the wildest and most inaccessible part of the Adirondacks. Surely Rondeau would have related that the winter of 1943–44 took a heavy toll of the deer herds, but by late spring 1946 they showed signs of making a fair comeback.

It has been over seven decades since the Boy Scouts of Paoli Troop 1 hiked to the safe Adirondack haven Noah John Rondeau called his City of Wigwams, but the memory has not diminished. What has stuck with them has been an unforgettable meeting with a special character who welcomed them into his woodland camp.

Noah's tending his plants. Rondeau's friends believed the hermit was an artist in his down-to-earth and organized poetry, in his well-managed flowerpots and vegetable garden, in his tepee-style wood piles and hermit clothing made from animal hides, in his brilliantly colored hand-formed fish lures and tied flies, in his detailed yearly diaries, and in his meticulous, clear, and elegant Spencerian penmanship. Courtesy Dr. Adolph G. Dittmar, Jr.

It's that simple legacy that has kept alight the flame of Noah John Rondeau's fame.

How could anyone not like a folk hero who volunteered he'd carry on a conversation with chipmunks and woodchucks just to have someone to talk to?

Rondeau might have had a shaggy, rough pine-bark appearance and his personal accomplishments in the mountains were simple, but he had a way

"Noah has time to cultivate flower and vegetable gardens around his shacks and in other clearings which survive from the days when the area was a thriving lumber center. He raises flowers and vegetables which do not appeal to marauding deer." From "Rondeau, Famed Adirondack Hermit, Has Many Friends in Southern Tier," September 20, 1946, *The Binghamton Press*. Courtesy Richard J. Smith from Rondeau's photo album.

with words that made him unforgettable: "And now in closing. Sunshine in tender green is at vernal best. A song sparrow jangles his small change among his musical notes. The dandelions are blooming and robins are whispering. Good luck to you and yours." —NJR

Eleanor Webb reported that she and Monty knew Rondeau and did not think of him as a celebrity but just an interesting old man who had led an unusually independent life, resorting to, for the most part, his own ingenuity.... "We know he was a spirited man, which some people found irritating, and somewhat hard to cope with, especially for those whose job it was to interfere with his independence. Yet there were those among those very people who became his good friends. With us, he was unfailingly courteous." Richard J. Smith from Rondeau's photo album

In the days prior to the arrival of the scouts, Noah entertained two close friends. On June 13, 1946, Noah led Ed Harmes and his son, Jack, to Couchsachraga Peak. Harmes's memories of many interesting conversation with the hermit included his intriguing, folksy charm when they got on a topic they were both passionate about. Courtesy Edward A. Harmes

Roy Snyder hams up how to enjoy a fiddle recital by the hermit. Roy recalled he was excited about his return to the hermitage. There was so much to catch up on. On June 16, 1946, they sat at the outside table on the hermit's "sun porch." Later, Noah fiddled while the forest critters danced to the hermit's variant of country fiddling. Courtesy Richard J. Smith from Rondeau's photo album

Big Dam, 1938. Courtesy Richard J. Smith from Rondeau's photo album

Noah John Rondeau's
"Cold River City"

This 1946 photograph shows the amount of water stored in Cold River Flow. It wasn't long after that a vast number of logs washed out the majority of **Big Dam.** Courtesy C.V. Latimer Jr., M.D.

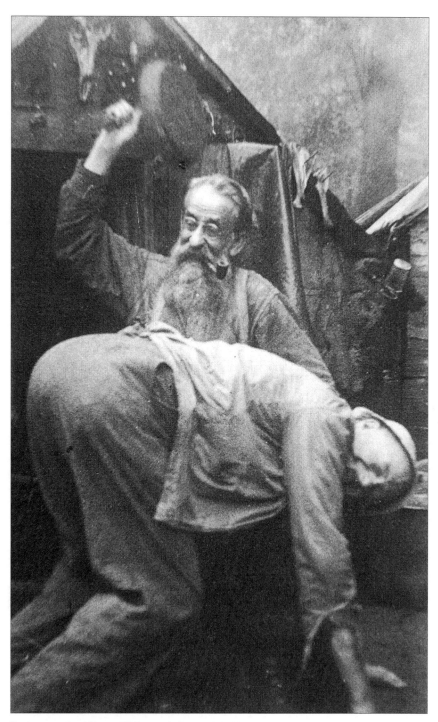

Noah warms the skillet on Ed Harmes in honor of his birthday. Courtesy E.A. Harmes

Johns Brook Lodge (JBL). August 1948. Dick Henderson worked at JBL as a hut boy for the last two weeks of the 1948 season. The reason he was there for such a short time was that he was filling in for his brother, Herbert J. Henderson (Hobey), who had to start his freshman year at Princeton early. Left to Right: Dick Terry, hut boy; Nubbins, the donkey ridden by the future Dr. John T. Carpenter, Jr. of Bryn Mawr, PA, an Adirondack 46er; Bill Patterson, hut master and Paoli Troop 1 scout master; unknown; Chris Knauth. Courtesy Richard A. Henderson

Dick's brief winter camping experience was no comparison to the many long winter nights Noah spent at the hermitage. Courtesy Harvey Carr

Winter's beauty. Cold River country, circa 1920. Photo by Richard Wood. Courtesy Inez Wood Buis

The scouts found Cold River's natural beauty worthy of pausing and locking into their memory.
Author's photo

Noah led the parade of scouts around the hermitage over a winding dirt path as he pointed out various places within his "city." Courtesy Bill Frenette

The scouts were given permission to look inside the Town Hall and Hall of Records huts.
Courtesy Richard J. Smith from Rondeau's photo album

Cold River's City of Wigwams. In Noah's solitary woods life, he was all-in-one mayor of Cold River, councilman, trustee, dog catcher, bird watcher, treasurer and town clerk. He often kidded he also reigned as king, even if he did occasionally fall under the suspicious eye of the Conservation Department, which ironically was the major cause of his fleeting fame and fortune during his late 1940s and early 1950s Sportsmen's Shows. Goff-Nelson Memorial Library, Tupper Lake, N.Y.

The hermit's bunk. Courtesy Richard J. Smith from Rondeau's photo album

Noah kept a detailed map tacked up on one wall. Today it is part of his collection housed in the Adirondack Experience's library collection. Courtesy Richard J. Smith from Rondeau's photo album

Dry food was kept in a variety of sealed glass jars. Courtesy Richard J. Smith from Rondeau's photo album

Noah called his system of preparing each season's supply of heating fuel "premeditated firewood."
Courtesy Richard J. Smith from Rondeau's photo album

Noah's method of drying firewood stacked wigwam-style added to Cold River Hill's mystique. Each tepee had a name: Beauty Parlor, Mrs. Rondeau's Kitchenette, Meat Wigwam, Pyramid of Giza, Summer Wigwam. Courtesy Peggy and Wayne Byrne

"During the summer, Rondeau constructs a series of large tepee-shaped structures around his cabin. These are made by sticking 25-foot logs in a circle so that the finished product resembles a tepee. Rondeau suspends large log chains with hooks dangling on the end. He hangs kettles on these?' —**Peggy Byrne.** Courtesy Richard J. Smith from Rondeau's photo album

From the late 1930s through the 1940s Noah had hung a hand-painted banner at the entrance and exit points to the hermitage. Courtesy Dr. Adolph G. Dittmar

OPPOSITE: Noah with a group of Boy Scouts at a Sportsmen's Show. Noah's nephew Burton Rondeau said, "The Conservation Department's stated goal was to use Uncle Noah to acquaint New York State's folks with the vast public wilderness domain—something Noah was proud of. Who better to talk about the glitter of mountain streams, the stands of beautiful hardwoods with green canopies that made walking beneath them like being in a city park, and the beauty of towering virgin pines rising high above the aromatic balsam and spruce? Noah could imitate the unforgettable calls of the owls and loons that break the night's silence, and when he described the sputters of frying brook trout, one could almost smell them." Noah could do that and more.

Burton continued: "Unquestionably he enjoyed the attention instant celebrity brought from adoring crowds." The so-called Mayor of Cold River was pictured on advertising posters. The very establishment about which he had so long spoken harshly laid a golden egg right in his lap, and he took quick advantage. To encourage onlookers to leave a donation, Noah borrowed seed money from Orville Betters and Hubert Toomey, state forest rangers, who were his guardians in New York City's late 1940s shows, to add to the hermit's false-bottomed pack basket filled with dollars and coins so spectators got the idea to toss in a donation for a poor bona fide hermit.

Noah was an articulate, witty, and authentic Adirondack character; the crowds loved him and his anecdotes and stories of the Cold River region, and he loved the attention. Radio shows scooped him up. His life story became a sensation. Courtesy Richard J. Smith from Rondeau's photo album

Noah and E.R. Harmes on a trail break. Noah spoke about his woods life. "There are rewards of living in the woods. Between Mountain Top and Ward Brook lean-tos there are many samples of rewards, the mountains, and valleys, rocks and hills, the frog in the mud-hole with his song, the woodpecker at work to get the sweetest worm, the cushions of living green moss often trimmed with redberries and ferns which invite the wanderer to rest and watch the picture show of clouds in the sky, rearranged every minute." Photo by Jack Harmes. Courtesy Edward R. Harmes

"Long before the 50-megaton bomb was created by scientists with an eye for the betterment of mankind, a young man of some 30 years, once a carpenter, once a barber, once a house painter, but a man with a lust against what he termed the 'slavery of industrialism,' put a pack on his sturdy back and walked solemnly into the Adirondacks.

"'The world,'" he said, "'is Big Business; it is getting too big; the pressure is on, and a man can't swing a double-bitted axe anymore and grow vegetables on a patch of land and make a living.'" — Barnett Fowler. Courtesy Earle Russell

N.J. Rondeau
at Cold River,
1934

His honor. Hermit-mayor Noah John Rondeau. From one of Noah's studio-produced promotional post cards.
Courtesy Peggy Byrne

The white sailor caps were an old tradition.

This picture was taken at Seward lean-to the next morning. The canopy has been taken down but things are drying over the fire.

Chapter 7

MINUTES AND PICTURES: COLD RIVER SIDE TRIP

Sunday, June 23: Another Sunday—the members of the expedition realized that the trip had been going for a whole week. Thinking of it made the boys feel like hardened veterans. Another clear cold morning and a fire was started and things got underway. It had been decided the previous night to omit the mountain climbing because the party was already a half day behind schedule and the bugs were very bad. The bugs would increase as they went farther into the wilderness.

The Cold River was little more than a large stream up near Rondeau's "city." It has boulders along its whole upper length.

This picture was taken through the trees on the way to Rondeau's with the river in the background.

Boys are [David] "Tinker" Aronson, "Boots" Clark, and Jeff Aronson. The expression on Tinker's face may be due to having carried the 70-pound food hamper.

More baking was done and after breakfast the packs were packed. The packs however were left behind when the party went up to visit old Noah John Rondeau, a hermit.

On the hike up the trail good speed was made because the only load carried was the lunch. In an hour the party was entering the gates of Cold River City, the hermitage of Mr. Rondeau. Mr. Rondeau was mayor and dogcatcher of the city, which consisted of two huts and about a half a dozen tepees made out of long logs, which were used for storage and other minor purposes.

The kitchen table at the Seward lean-to. The reason for "Boots" Clark sticking out his tongue is not clear. In the background is Peter Schultz.

Mr. Rondeau was there to greet us when we came into his city. He was just as the boys imagined a hermit should be. He was an old man of about 62 with a great stoop that made him very short. He greeted Bill as an old friend and then shook hands with all of us. He made the party welcome and they sat down in the center of his camp while he talked. After a short time, he let the boys examine the whole camp. Gifts of tobacco, lard and coffee were given to him, for which he was very grateful. He brought out his guest book and let the boys sign it. Then he wrote messages in the minutes book, which are in the back of this book. He also showed the boys many of his photographs and cards which all his hiker friends send him. Included were some showing Bill Patterson visiting him on earlier occasions. Mr. Rondeau also gave the boys a small present in the form of a beautiful partridge feather for each one.

Noah Rondeau sits by a crude bench while he writes messages in the boys' books. He had wonderful handwriting skills.

Here the boys are being shown something about Cold River City by Bill Patterson.

As Mr. Rondeau talked, the interested boys soon got glimpses of his character. Eccentric he may have been, but he was every inch a gentleman and also was rather intelligent. He told the boys his reasons for being a hermit. His savings had been wiped out when the Philadelphia Building and Loan Association collapsed and shortly after that his house burned down. For these reasons he got fed up with the filthy capitalists and moved out where he could be close to nature. He also had very definite ideas about world politics, which he told the boys about.

Mr. Rondeau had another dislike and that was of the game protectors. He did however like very much the rangers.

When the boys examined his city and his property, they also got an idea of how Mr. Rondeau lived out in the wilderness. He lived off the land a lot, although he goes to a town 20 miles away around Christmas time and gets supplies. The many friends who visit him even in the winter always bring presents. He traps animals for their pelts and meat. He used to hunt with his huge 80-pound bow but now because of age does it mostly with a gun. Once each year he kills a bear. He also kills deer. The hermit's huts have bones of these animals on the fronts of them. He showed the boys his big knife.

Later on, the cooks prepared lunch and he ate with us. Mr. Rondeau's life may be meager and not very useful, but he enjoys it and the country he lives it in. After lunch Mr. Rondeau posed for several pictures by himself and with the boys. Mr. Rondeau has a very old fiddle which he showed us which he can play well. Unfortunately, it was out of commission at the moment with a broken string.

After the pictures had been taken, he shook each boy's hand and bid us farewell. His parting comment to Dick Henderson was, "Have a good time with those pretty young women down at Philadelphia." Mr. Rondeau never was married but everything that goes wrong about Cold River City is blamed on the mythical Mrs. Rondeau.

Rondeau and the boys in Cold River City.

The party hiking back to the canoes. Notice the tumplines to help support the loads.

During one of the many rests which the party took along the way everyone swatted mosquitos and black flies, which came in droves.

This view shows all but a few of the tepees of Cold River City.

Bill Patterson greets Mr. Rondeau. Bill and Rondeau are old friends from the pre-war days when Bill climbed the neighboring mountains with boys from Camp Passumpsic.

The party poses with Mr. Rondeau with the Cold River City in the background.

Mr. Rondeau is a genial host and offered to show the boys all his possessions. Here he is showing them his many photographs. "As I leaned over Noah's back to see what was in the box, Noah John turned his head to me, and spoke to me in such a calm way that I knew he knew me, and that I knew him and that everything would be OK. I left the hermit's camp with calm and peace, and energy, too." — Dick Henderson.

Mr. Rondeau assumed this pose immediately when we informed him that we wanted to take pictures of him. He is still very active and swings his axe like a true woodsman.

Standing Left to Right: Herbert J. Henderson, William Z. McLear, Richard A. Henderson, Robert T. Ives, John "Jack" Holtzapple, David Aronson, Edgar S. Kennedy, Jr., John Clutz, John Aronson (behind J. Clutz), Donald I. Lamont, Peter Schultz. Sitting Left to Right: Niles Beeson, Paul Clark, Stuart Horton, Noah John Rondeau, William C. Patterson, Scoutmaster, and taking this photograph, Scout and Trip Photographer George M. Aman 3rd.

The night after visiting the hermit, the boys returned from Seward lean-to and slept at the Latham Pond lean-to near Shattuck Clearing.

At Latham Pond lean-to a few of the fellows unaccustomed to hiking developed blisters. Here Bill McLear is treating Dick Henderson for a blister on his foot.

After bidding him goodbye they half ran back to the Seward lean-to where after a short rest they pushed on down the trail to Latham Pond lean-to. As the utility bag was being unpacked it was discovered that the pliers and the axe files were missing. After conducting a search in the other bags, Bill McLear and Bob Ives volunteered to return to Seward lean-to and search for them. After getting an extra chocolate bar they set out and after encountering many bugs at the former campsite they succeeded in finding the axe file. The pliers were later found in the bag containing the reflector ovens.

Dinner that night included such choice items as rice with molasses and Spam. (The third night in a row for Spam.) It was however topped off by a delicious apple pie made from dried apples and baked in the reflector ovens.

While attempting to find a good rock on which to wash the dishes, George Aman slipped and fell partially into the stream, losing the huge pile of pans and silverware which he had been carrying. Most of the articles however were retrieved from the swift steam after a bit of wading etc. At this lean-to there were also many bugs including a multitude of the horrible midges.

Later after dinner a few boys went swimming in the Cold River. Also, the cooking detail for the next day made some corn bread for the next breakfast. Then when it became time to go to bed, the boys all invented original

This picture was natural and un-posed. It happened at Latham Pond after many of the boys tried putting molasses on their rice.

means of avoiding the midges. Since they flew right through mosquito netting, regular cloth was required, which made breathing rather difficult. After much contriving, the boys finally turned in and taps was blown.

Another view of Lathan Pond camp. This view shows the very rocky ground. The boys are wearing mosquito netting.

Chapter 8

ON TO RAQUETTE FALLS AND BEYOND

Monday, June 24: The boys arose early this morning because they were still behind schedule and they hoped to catch up and get to their regular destination for this night, which was Axton lean-to. The day's traveling would then include four-miles of hiking and finally uncaching the canoes and packing them, and then 13 miles including a portage.

The boys waded down the Cold River from Latham Pond until it became too deep. One or two boys fell in, including Bill Patterson.

Jeff Aronson, one of the cooks, displays some very tasty chocolate muffins. They were baked at Latham Pond.

Another reason for the early arising was the midges. It was at Latham Pond that the first verses of the camp song were invented. This song includes a very true one about the bugs.

Boots Clark walking through a portage at Raquette Falls. He is wearing a head net to avoid the bugs. Also shown is Stuart Horton, the smallest member of the group. He is probably going through for the second time carrying odds and ends left behind.

The party stopped at Raquette Falls instead of Axton lean-to on Monday night. Here Peter Schult (center) makes a fire in the fireplace.

While Tinker Aronson and Niles Beeson explored an old logging trail to try to find an easier way to return to the canoes, camp was taken down and the packs packed. At ten-fifteen the hikers headed down the trail on the north side of the river. They followed it until it petered out and then started bushwhacking. The going became worse and worse until the party was making almost no headway. At last, in exasperation they came to the bank of the river and voted to try wading down the river bed. With dungarees rolled up and shoes remaining on, they stepped into the stream and walking on sand bars as much as possible proceeded down the stream. During the infrequent rests the boys examined their heels, which were coming off, and poured the water out of their shoes. The water became deeper as they continued. Finally, at one especially deep spot, going over large stones Bill Patterson slipped into the water and sat down. The food hamper he was carrying became wet. Also John Clutz, Jack Holtzapple, Bob Ives, Tinker Aronson and Peter Schultz fell in to a greater or lesser extent. After these mishaps the party took to the land and finding a trail they quickly walked to the place where the canoes were cached. Everything was dragged to the water's edge and the cooks opened the lunch bag and began preparing lunch. Meanwhile wet articles including the food hamper were examined and fixed. Packs were repacked with the material in cache for the portage. Then lunch was served. The canoes were gotten over a bar and into the deep water, then the boys resumed their journey, thinking that paddling was much nicer than wading.

This picture was taken at Latham Pond. Boots Clark and Don Lamont are washing dishes in the Cold River.

Upon coming to the joining of the Cold River and the Raquette River they turned downstream on the Raquette River. After paddling for six miles they came to the portage by the falls on the Raquette River. The portage was a half mile of hilly traveling to calm water. They then paddled five minutes till the Raquette Falls camp came in view. It was decided to stay there instead of going five miles further to the Axton camp. The landing was very muddy but the canoes were unloaded and camp was soon pitched. While the cooks prepared supper, several boys went in swimming and found that the current in the seemingly sluggish stream was rather powerful.

All the boys who went in swimming rejoiced to find that they had left the midges and black flies behind. Soon many mosquitos came to make up the deficiency. Dinner featured more Spam and dried vegetables. Later on a cake was baked in honor of J.C. Clutz's birthday which had happened several days ago. A big day awaited the boys on the next day so all retired rather early.

The Raquette Falls camp.

This picture shows the lean-to shelters we used for our Raquette Falls camp.

Chapter 9

INDIAN CARRY TO THE SARANACS

Tuesday, June 25: The boys arose early today because they had to travel many miles. After breakfast the packs were packed quickly and the party set out. Five easy miles of paddling down the Raquette River were quickly put behind them as the boys played a game to see who could swat the most dragon flies. Fortunately, many of the bad insects were not around.

They then turned off the river into Stony Creek Inlet which turned out to be another winding swampy area. Then they came out into Stony Creek Ponds. After much searching in which there was much talk about maps

This is an extraordinary canoe shelter built by J.C. Clutz at Raquette Falls. He thought it was going to rain which it did not.

John Clutz carrying a pack through Bartlett Carry between Upper and Middle Saranac Lakes. The pack is not the biggest one carried by him as it only has three duffels on it and weighs 65 pounds.

A canoe on Middle Saranac Lake with Ampersand Mountain in the background.

being left in packed duffel bags when they might be needed, the town of Coreys was found. It consisted of exactly one building. This was the ramshackle post office. Here mail was received and the last of the food packages. After repacking the food supplies, lunch was prepared and quickly eaten.

Here the group is returning from Saranac Lake town with food and other purchases.

The biggest, 6'4", and the smallest boy, Jeff Aronson and Stuart Horton.

Here at Eagle Island, Boots Clark is administering a haircut to Tinker Aronson. The razor was used efficiently but without much artistic ability.

Then the party started on one of the longest carries of the trip, known as Indian Carry. This portage from the nearest point of the Raquette River would have been three miles but by going through the Stony Creek Ponds they cut it to a mile and a quarter. After completing this portage, they set out and quickly crossed the lake to the Bartlett Carry into Middle Saranac Lake. This carry was completed in record time. The portage was very short but it was finished in 25 minutes including packing the canoes. They got water from an old boat house faucet and proceeded down a short inlet into Middle Saranac Lake. This was a beautiful lake and the boys saw Mount Ampersand and thought of climbing it later on.

After traversing Middle Saranac Lake to its other end they found the outlet into the Saranac River. This was a winding swampy stream with markers every few feet for the large boats. After going a short distance, the canoes came to the locks. There were old, hand-operated ones made of wood and cared for by an old man. We were lowered about three feet and marveling at modern science (the locks were built in 1890) we proceeded down the Saranac River and into Lower Saranac Lake. After finally finding Eagle Island, which was the night's destination, the navigator sailed down the north side searching for the shelter. After some of the canoes had sailed completely around the island the shelter was found, contrary to directions, on the south side. It was a huge rock about 200 feet high which was called Tom's Rock. On the top of this rock commanding a wonderful view was the shelter, a beautiful stone one with a nice bronze plaque on the side.

The time was late, about 6:30 and the boys were very tired. They had come almost 20 miles including a mile and a half of portage. It was the greatest distance covered in one day during the whole trip. A late supper was cooked and while everyone pulled up the canoes the last baking was done. Dinner was eaten happily as everyone admired the view of the lake. After supper everyone went to bed.

Chapter 10

EAGLE ISLAND THREE-DAY LAYOVER

Wednesday June 26: Since the troop was staying in this camp for three days there was no necessity to arise early and so breakfast was not eaten until about ten o'clock. After breakfast everyone did a large amount of washing of clothes. The washing was done on boulders by the shore of the lake. After it was finished and the clothes were hung on a line the group all dressed in regular Scout uniform, and went into the nearby town. This involved a mile and a half of paddling and the same amount of hiking after reaching the dock on the main shore.

With more time to prepare it the food became very well cooked and more elaborate than on the journey. Here they are being served breakfast.

As the boys walked along the road into the town they were happy to be back in civilization after six days in bleak wilderness. After reaching the town, which was discovered to be a large one, all dispersed to complete the tasks of supply, to have shoes repaired and last but not least, to eat as much ice cream as was possible. At four-thirty after two hours in the town, the group met at the municipal building and packed the purchases of food etc. on the frames. Here the mail orderly distributed mail that he had gotten at the post office. They hastened to depart from the town because the weather seemed to promise a storm before night fall. After reaching the canoes and loading them they shoved off and began battling the strong headwind and high waves that had come up.

This picture may give some idea of the reasons for the popularity of the campsite at Eagle Island.

Progress was very slow and when the party finally reached the camp the bow men were almost soaked. Everyone agreed that it had been the toughest headwind of the trip. The boys who had stayed at the camp related some of the things they had done which included trying to rig a sail for a canoe and giving a haircut to Tinker Aronson.

Soon a delicious dinner of all fresh food was cooking and some of the boys went in for a swim. The dinner of steak and fresh vegetables was eaten with much relish but without the grain of salt eaten earlier in the trip because they had run out of this useful article. To top off this fine dinner a delicious apple pie was baked by the cooks. This was also enjoyed very much and many

This is how the lake looked from the lean-to high above the water. The boy sitting on the fireplace is Hobey Henderson.

of the boys thought that this was the best meal of the trip. After the cleanup detail had finished their unpleasant task the boys gathered out on the point of the rock and while the night slowly descended they had a good song fest. After this everyone went to bed. Taps was sounded at 10:45 and the boys slept well as the strong wind had taken away all the mosquitoes.

The boys are washing their dirty clothes after the five days in the mountains. In the background is the base of Tom's Rock.

Chapter 11

COMPETITION CANOE MEET

hursday, June 27: The boys got up at seven o'clock and while a few enjoyed an early dip breakfast was quickly prepared. After breakfast seven boys got in uniform and returned again to the town to purchase the remaining supplies for the trip. While they were gone the rest of the boys rested, read, swam, and did anything else they wanted. Don Lamont and Tinker Aronson swam over to a nearby island.

When the boys returned from the town at 2:30 a late lunch was eaten and then the boys rested for a while as a few planned the canoe meet. At four o'clock this meet was held which included splashing fights, gunwale pumping, and canoe tilting. The grand finale was a general free-for-all in which anything was allowed. This was quickly ended with all but one canoe sunk. After a late dinner three boys went out fishing in a canoe. Soon all went to bed.

Here the boys are having a gunwhale pumping race. The canoes are propelled by jumping up and down on the rear gunwhale.

This picture shows the top half of Tom's Rock with the camp on the top.

Here the boys are having a splashing fight at Eagle Island. Notice the bucket being used to fill the opponent's canoe.

Chapter 12

FINAL DAY ON UPPER SARANAC

Friday, June 28: This day reveille was at 5:30 for again the boys had to break camp and move on to their final camp on Upper Saranac. They hoped to cover this distance of 16 miles including one short portage by lunch time. The packs were packed and since too much food had been bought at Saranac Lake village each pack had to hold four duffels. This made the weight of them about 85 pounds.

By shortly after eight the canoes were packed and ready to leave. A calm had set in and the water was as smooth as glass. Lower Saranac Lake was traversed quickly and soon the canoes were again entering the locks on the Saranac River. After being lifted up they continued through the swampy area and out

Here are the canoes on the last day of traveling. This shot was taken on Lower Saranac Lake.

on Middle Saranac Lake. By this time the sun had come out brightly and many of the boys took off their shirts. After going the length of this lake they came to Bartlett Carry. The canoes were beached and the boys shouldered canoes and 85-pound packs and set off over their last portage.

At the finish of the last portage chocolate was eaten and the canoes set out across Upper Saranac Lake. Trying to find a campsite on this lake consumed much time and since there was no erected shelter here it was a hard task. Lunch was eaten at a point on the lake and then the canoes went up Fish Creek inlet into Fish Creek Bay and finally with the aid of a ranger the boys found a campsite through an inlet on Follensby Clear Pond. Here was a deserted tent frame shelter which the boys covered with their pup tent halves. This camp was about 150 yards from the highway. Here were swarms of mosquitos to greet the group and the superiority of the previous camp to this one was evident. Supper was cooked and eaten rapidly and Mr. Krick appeared with his son. They ate with us and after supper all went in swimming. After

This picture, taken late the first evening at Upper Saranac, shows just about nothing.

swimming, seven of the boys went out in canoes to sleep for the night. They did this to escape the bugs and were very successful. The canoes were tied together and anchored. Soon taps was blown.

This shot of the camp at Follensby Clear Pond near Upper Saranac shows the old tent frame used as a shelter.

Dams form feeding and resting places for fish

Chapter 13

FINAL DAY

Saturday, June 29: The boys arose at about 7:30 on this the last day of their trip. After breakfast a few boys went shopping for food in Mr. Krick's car while the rest of the boys washed or fished in the pond. After the boys returned, lunch was eaten and then everyone got in uniform to take the canoes to the express office to be shipped back to Rivett's Boat Livery. They paddled out Fish Creek Inlet and across Upper Saranac Lake to a stream which they had been told would be navigable to near the station. After going about a half of the distance the stream became impassible and the canoes were hauled through the woods and taken by car to the station. After tagging them and storing them they all departed to the Saranac Inn and did some shopping. Then they returned

This picture is also of the last campsite.

to the camp and prepared supper. Several of the cars were around by this time. After supper a last campfire was held and Mr. Krick gave a short talk. Then everybody went to bed.

Here the duffels and equipment are being packed in the cars Sunday morning.

Logs from a trapper fire will make a reflector

Bill Patterson, the leader of the trip, leaves at Whitehall N.Y. to become a counselor at Camp Passumsic in Vermont.

Chapter 14

HOMEWARD BOUND

Sunday, June 30: After a torturing night with the mosquitos, reveille was blown at 4:45. The boys jumped out of bed quickly and went in for a short dip. Then a hasty breakfast was eaten and the duffels were packed and taken out to the cars where everything was packed. The campsite was policed for the last time and all gathered out on the highway. After a short delay the car started on the 400-mile journey at the hour of 6 A.M. The four car drivers were Mr. Krick, Mr. Davis, Mr. and Mrs. Holtzapple, and Mr. and Mrs. Aronson. Mr. Krick let Don Lamont off at Lake Placid where he got a train to his farm job, and he also let off Bill Patterson nearby to go to Camp Passumsic. The journey home was uneventful but many of the boys listened to the atomic bomb explosion over the radio. The cars arrived home between six and seven o'clock.

NOAH JOHN RONDEAU
CITY MAYOR
COLD RIVER CITY

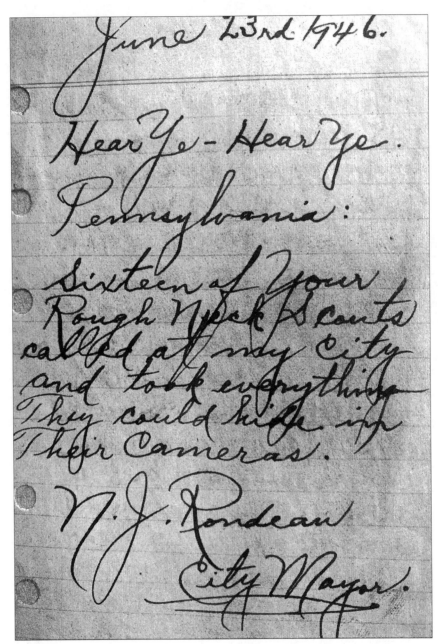

June 23rd 1946.

Hear Ye - Hear Ye.

Pennsylvania :

Sixteen of Your
Rough Neck Scouts
called at my City
and took everything
They could hide in
Their Cameras.

N. J. Rondeau
City Mayor.

Mr. Rondeau wrote the comical message in the minutes book when we visited him.

This picture was taken of Mr. Rondeau as he chopped wood. He is a very good woodsman.

BE FIRST CLASS

Be first class—The first words that appear in the Handbook for Boys published in 1948 by the National Council of Boy Scouts of America.

They say scouting "builds character." Maybe it even influences one throughout one's life. Through my experience, I believe it does.

Among many other skills, Troop 1's 1946 classic canoe paddle taught the scouts paddling techniques. For example, the stern man does the steering while the bow man keeps look-out for snags, and selects the quiet parts of the river. He warns the stern man of rocks and logs ahead. In quickwater, the bow of the canoe will usually float away from a rock; it's the stern that must be kept clear.

In the stern position, the paddler turns the blade of the paddle at the end of a stroke with an outward twist when the canoe has a tendency to turn off

Near the foot of Long Lake, where the paddler in the stern position turns the canoe toward the mouth of Cold River. Courtesy C.V. Latimer Jr., M.D.

OPPOSITE: **His Honor, the Mayor of Cold River Flow.** Photograph by Edward Hudowalski. Courtesy Grace Hudowalski

The Boy Scouts *Handbook For Boys* is an indispensable resource. 1946 Boy Scouts Handbook

course in the direction opposite to the side one is paddling on. This pushes the stern over and makes the craft head straight. If it turns the other way, he takes a little harder stroke, with a flat blade. One learns to keep it headed right without disturbing the even, steady rhythm of paddling.

Canoe-camping was only one of myriad fun and adventurous activities Paoli Troop 1 pursued that afforded the opportunity to aim toward being first class. The expedition gave the boys the occasion to practice any number of skills, to be prepared at any moment to do their duty, and to face danger, if necessary, to help others.

End of the line. Paddlers reach a point where Cold River cannot be paddled further upstream.
Courtesy C.V. Latimer Jr., M.D.

I imagine that enjoying the out-of-doors and respect for nature and each other would top the list if the Paoli scouts were asked to sum up their paddling adventure in one sentence.

Lean-tos along Adirondack waterways are an important resource. Today the Adirondack Mountain Club has established a system of lean-to volunteers to help take care of the log shelters. Photo by Ed Fynmore. Courtesy Town of Webb Historical Association P5733

Adirondack Mountain Club's Johns Brook Lodge, August 1947. Seated on the floor to the right is JBL hutmaster Bill Patterson, who was one of Paoli Troop 1's Old Forge to Saranac Lake Canoe Trip leaders in 1946. Standing directly behind Bill is Herbert J. (Hobey) Henderson, a hut boy at JBL in both 1947 and 1948. Standing to the far right is Chris Knauth. Seated on the railing to Hobey's right is Dick Terry and his family. Courtesy Richard Henderson

RAQUETTE FALLS, THE LAST FRONTIER IN THE ADIRONDACKS

R uddy-cheeked, white haired, vivacious, cultured, gallant, George Morgan would have been thoroughly at home in a dowager's drawing room on Park Avenue, and she would have been charmed by him. Yet it is doubtful if he had graced such surroundings for a quarter of a century before his death.

My recollections of the people at Raquette Falls before the spring of 1925 are very vague. Then one day in June, Jack Olwine and I found George Morgan in charge. He invited us up to his log cabin on the knoll. As we talked, our eyes were dazzled by the great stack of books, shelved clear to the ceiling. We hadn't expected to find a private library of such dimensions that far back in the Adirondack wilderness. And the years held other surprises.

When the old two-story house burned down, George replaced it with a replica of a lumber camp. It was an affair of huge logs, containing living room, dining room, bedrooms, bath and a huge kerosene refrigerator in the kitchen. A meal in the dining room was served with the éclat of a first class hotel—lovely dishes, waiter in white jacket, and all the trimmings. In front of the open porch was a well-kept lawn. A canoe paddle bearing the legend "Raquette Falls Lodge" was suspended between two young pines.

But the biggest surprise was George himself. We presently learned that he had retired from a law practice in New York and that he and his wife were living at Raquette Falls the year around. He lived there alone in later years, except for a couple who worked for him during the summer. He was well past 70, and it seemed strange and unfortunate that he should be alone, miles from the nearest road and house, especially during Adirondack winters.

He had a passionate love for the place where he lived. I'll never forget my last evening with him. He and I were alone in his cabin. We sipped a little, talked some, and I read to him from DeVoto's *The Year of Decision*. (Since the preceding December, because of increasing blindness, he had been unable to read). It was late as we stepped off the porch out into the gorgeous moonlight.

George Morgan at Raquette Falls. Photo taken the day Billy Burger and Jack Olwine visited Raquette Falls. Courtesy Billy Burger

Spread out below us were the lodge and clearing with deep woods banked all around. A luminous mist rose from falls and rapids, and the only sound was the gentle murmur of water running over rocks. George took my arm as he said, "Can there be anything in the world more beautiful than this?" He could see it but dimly, but how he could feel the beauty of that night!

What courage he had! The winter before he died, though he had high blood pressure, a double hernia, and very poor vision, he cut and drew all his wood. Rather, he cut and rode the logs a half-mile down a winding road on a sled of skis he had rigged up. Once the contraption hit a tree and he almost broke his neck. But he laughed as he told about it.

How he could laugh and quote poetry and prose by the hour, and what stories he could tell! Here is a sample.

One day when a case he was trying in a New York court was recessed for a while, he went into a neighboring courtroom to pass the time. A man was up for bigamy. He was a little man, weighing possibly 100 pounds. The first witness against him was a big, florid woman with tawny hair, baby blue eyes, and an immense bosom. As George said, "When she sat on the witness chair, she spilled over." Yes, she was married to this man. Any evidence? Yes, the marriage certificate. It was passed around and seemed okay. The next witness was built like a lead pencil. Yes, she was married to the defendant. Any evidence? Yes, a marriage certificate. It, too, was passed around.

Then the big and handsome lawyer for the little man got up, and placing his hands on the head of his client, said, "Now, Henry the Eighth, it's your turn." On the stand it was evident he didn't know the score. The judge quickly charged the jury. They retired and were soon back. It seemed like a closed case. The judge smiled as he asked for the verdict, but was furious when the response was "not guilty." All the members were polled. Same result. There was nothing for the judge to do but dismiss the case. On the way out, George sidled up to a couple of the jurors. As he had suspected, "Now, Henry the Eighth, it's your turn" did the trick. George said it was one of the cleverest stunts he had ever seen done in a courtroom.

Once when we were spending a memorable night at the lodge, George told us how he had rescued two damsels in distress the year before. One day he heard a call for help from across the river just below the last rapids. He rowed over in his skiff and found two girls standing on a rock with little on but shorts and bras. Because of high water they had missed the carry a mile above, had been sucked into the rapids, and had lost the canoe and all their duffle. Characteristically, George fed and clothed them and gave them money to get home. Their chief worry was the canoe which they had rented at Old Forge. Here again George came to the rescue with a suggestion. Said he, "If you write the canoe people that you've lost the canoe, they'll bill you for 60 to 70 dollars. But if you write that you've had a wonderful trip and despite the fact that it leaks a little, you've fallen in love with the canoe and want to buy it, they'll charge only 25 dollars." They followed George's advice, and that is precisely what happened!

George used to say Raquette Falls is the "last frontier in the Adirondacks." While there are a few other places as remote, or even more so, it is 17 miles by boat to Long Lake, the nearest village up river and lake in one direction, and Tupper Lake is 25 miles by water downstream. There is no road or even summer trail to the falls. In winter you can snowshoe out to the post office in a house at Coreys, but it's almost eight miles and plenty rugged.

Mrs. Billy and I had said goodbye to the Bryans on the dock of Plumley Camp near the foot of Long Lake. They were very close friends of George Morgan and had been spending a few days with him. Now they were on their way to their home in New York, where Mr. Bryan was a ship builder.

We stepped into our canoe and pushed off for the eight-mile run to Raquette Falls Carry, the walk across, and the visit with George we had been promising ourselves. It was a gorgeous mid- September day, mild and sunny.

As we crossed the clearing to the lodge, we noticed the flag wasn't up—an indication that George was alone. The front door had never had a lock on it. We went in and started back through the dining room, but stopped suddenly on the threshold. On the table was an unfinished meal—steak and all the trimmings. Three places had been set, evidently for dinner the night before. On the floor was a blanket with something under it. Then we saw this note on a chair: "Thursday, 6:30 AM. We have gone to Coreys to notify authorities. T.H. Rome."

"Is it murder?" flashed through my mind. We went back into the kitchen. There were three empty soup plates and a pot of cold coffee on the stove. While Mrs. Billy walked back to the porch, I hurried up to George's private cabin on the hill. No sign of him there. Back at the lodge, I finally screwed up my courage to look under the blanket. Sure enough, there was George, dead. I joined Mrs. Billy on the porch. The lunch we tried to eat tasted as dry as sawdust.

Coreys is eight miles from the Lodge by canoe and road. Whoever Rome was, he and whoever was with him had left six hours before. Someone should be showing up soon. We sat in the lean-to out front and watched the river below the falls.

Raquette Falls headquarters, 1938. Courtesy Phil Wolff

Finally it was 2:30, and we decided that we should start the nine miles up river and lake to Plumley's to telephone the Bryans in New York and others, for who could tell what had happened to "Rome" on the way down. I wrote a note and left it with the other on the chair. As we came out of the lodge, we saw a boat being rowed up to the landing. I recognized the oarsman as Mr. Bryan, to whom we had said goodbye in the morning. In the boat were the coroner from Tupper Lake and Ross Freeman of Coreys. Another boat followed with the embalmer and Mrs. Bryan.

The story was soon told. Despite his near blindness and other infirmities, George Morgan had driven his own boat the tricky six and a half miles to

Axton the day before, walked the mile and half to the post office, phoned for a taxi to Tupper Lake ten miles away, spent the day there and returned, arriving at the lodge with supplies in the late afternoon. As he was resting on the porch, a young couple, the Romes, whom he had never seen before, came by with their packs. He invited them to spend the night. I can imagine what he said: "I've just bought a fine steak in Tupper. Let's eat it together." So it was a gay trio that got the meal.

They set the table with the lodge's fine dishes, lit the big lamp, and served and ate the soup. After George had carved the steak and they had started to eat it, he said, "Excuse me," rose from the table, started for the living room, lay down on the floor and was dead in five minutes. Of course, the Romes couldn't eat and I don't believe they slept, for none of the beds had been used. At daybreak they started down the river for help.

The funeral and burial were next day, and of course we stayed. Since the men who came from Coreys seemed to be busy at other tasks and since Mr. Bryan, who it turned out was executor of George's estate, wanted to have the funeral promptly, he and I dug the grave the next morning out in front of George's cabin. The shipbuilder and little I must have presented quite a spectacle as we spelled each other every five or ten minutes, and how George would have chuckled if he could have seen us!

While the twenty friends of George's who gathered in the living room for the funeral were keenly sorry he had gone, we couldn't really mourn, for his death, we knew, was a welcome release from serious physical infirmities, old age, sorrow, loneliness, and misfortune. We had been greatly concerned about his living there alone, especially in winter, and had tried to get him to leave, but he loved this beautiful deep woods spot too much.

Now a tablet set in a boulder marking the last resting place of his mortal remains, bears this inscription: George E. Morgan, 1870–1944. Scholar, Woodsman, Friend, Resident of This Place 1919–1944. And George Morgan's spirit will hover above the spot as long as the river runs over the falls, for to him it was heaven.

SHATTUCK CLEARING AND FOREST RANGER LUCIUS RUSSELL

Retracing Paoli Troop 1's route to Shattuck Clearing and on to the hermit's river-top bluff in the 21st Century would seem more wild-like today.

Canoeing in from Long Lake, one enters the Raquette River, proceeds on down to the mouth of Cold River and turns upstream past Calkins Brook lean-to, caches the canoe and follows an old heavily overgrown trail along the river for three miles to Shattuck's Clearing and the forested site of the former ranger's station. Here the Northville-Placid trail intersects and is followed upstream past Natural Dam or Miller's Falls (three miles), and on to the former Big Dam (another three miles) and Rondeau's bluff where he had erected a "Gate to the City."

The interior ranger station at Shattuck Clearing was burned down in 1975. Shortly afterward the truck bridge that spanned Cold River was dismantled. The Clearing had been Ranger Lucius "Lou" Russell's assignment for five days and six nights a week from 1944 until 1956. In 1956, he suffered a fatal stroke on the trail during a trip to his home in Long Lake with Sue, his Airedale.

During Paoli Troop 1's June 1946 lunch stopover at Shattuck Clearing, Ranger Russell was not there. It was in July of 1946 while returning to Big Horn camp at Shattuck Clearing with Victor Baumister that Lou had his first stroke.

There is little evidence of the ranger's station today.

In the interest of preserving a bit of Shattuck Clearing history, William "Billy" H. Burger's story about the once well-known ranger's camp appears here. The article first appeared in *North Country Life* Summer 1950 magazine.

Burger, a resident of Westport, N.Y. acted as Associate Editor of the magazine. He authored a long-running "The Adirondacker" column for *The Record-Post*, Au Sable Forks, N.Y. throughout

World War II. Billy and Lillian Burger counted Noah John Rondeau, the famed Adirondack hermit, among their closest life-long friends.

Noah with a post-Christmas group at Burgers' The Pipemakers home in Westport, N.Y. December 29, 1939. The Burgers and their guests display their fancy long-stem clay pipes. Front row. Left to right: George Sausville, Hazel Gibson, Lillian Burger, unknown. Back row, Left to right: unknown, Noah J. Rondeau, Billy Burger, and Katherine Kuhfahl. Courtesy Jean Burger Cushman

"Shattuck's Clearing is about four miles up Cold River from Calkins Creek and a little farther from Plumley's near the foot of Long Lake. One day we noticed a new cabin had been built for the resident forest ranger. It was a very good looking and substantial log job. Then a while later there was a new ranger who more than matched the cabin. He invited us inside, told us to help ourselves to jam and peanut butter and in general to make ourselves at home.

"Good looking, smooth-shaven, and soft spoken, he somehow seemed a bit out of place, but that was a very fleeting impression. Behind the bland and gracious façade was as much of the real stuff as the old Adirondacks ever saw. For instance, when a big boy came bounding down the trail from Seward Lean-to at dusk one night to get help for a man who had nearly drowned, he ran back with the boy and stood by most of the night (I know about this, for I was the man). One hot July morning this ranger collapsed under a fifty-pound pack on the trail going up to Plumley's, but he kept on to the cabin by dint of sheer grit.

"After I got acquainted with Lucius Russell, I could understand why his cabin was such a popular hang-out. Every time I went by, there seemed to be someone there, and the stories over the coffee cups were pretty tall. After he had his stroke, I found Deputy State Conservation Commissioner Vic Skiff and his boy and Clayt Seagears, Educational Director of the Conservation Department, making themselves very much at home here one morning on my way up to visit Noah Rondeau. One of Lucius' city pals, a brain specialist in New York, thought so much of him that he flew to Long Lake to look him over and later had him down to New York for an operation. That's the kind of guy he is.

Seward Lean-to as it appeared in 1926. Courtesy C.V. Latimer Jr. M.D.

"Lucius Russell was born at Long Lake. Anyone meeting him now is amazed to learn that he finished school with the sixth grade, for he could readily pass as a college graduate. Most of his life has been spent guiding, caretaking, and logging. It was not until eight years ago that he became a state employee. His first job was that of observer at Owl's Head Mountain (the Long Lake one) and in 1944 he became Forest ranger at Shattuck's Clearing. Except for his 8 months illness, he's been on the job since, looking out for fires in his valley.

In addition to maintaining a mountain fire station headquarters, with portable gasoline pump and other equipment, and sleeping quarters for fire-fighting crews, he keeps the eleven-mile trail between Plumley's and the Dam open and the lean-tos in good condition.

"His attractive, well-kept home is located across the bridge in Long Lake on the road to Tupper. When the woods are well wet down, Lucius gets out to the house over weekends and sometimes in between. He commutes by kicker the seven miles from Plumley's to the village.

"Since his stroke he has had the help of a jackass to carry supplies, which like all worthy jackasses adds to the fun of living. A dog and pet deer, who pry into his private life early evenings, keep him from getting too lonesome. There's a tiny but fertile garden near the cabin. Lucius Russell's life is pretty full of a number of things."

Conservation Department jeep at Shattuck Clearing, circa 1950s. Author's Collection

Earle F. Russell shared, on November 1, 1950, on a return trek to Shattuck Clearing, "Dad encoun-
tered a not-so-friendly 500-pound black bear. Dad won that one, defending himself and his dog,
Sue. He gave the hide to Noah John Rondeau and the meat to Reverend Ray Morgan, pastor of the
Wesleyan Church in Long Lake where he was a member." Courtesy Earle F. Russell

Noah John Rondeau asleep in Big Horn Camp, Shattuck Clearing. Courtesy C.V. Latimer Jr., M.D.

Big Horn Camp, Shattuck Clearing, Summer 1950. Courtesy Ed Kornmeyer

"I'll always remember the red geraniums planted in Shattuck Clearing's window boxes, the scenic view of distant mountains, the split-rail fence, and how welcoming the interior ranger's greeting to m was when I first saw the interior ranger post in the summer of 1971."—William J. "Jay" O'Hern.
Author's photo

Noah hired a Saranac Lake photographer to create a post card series of hermit images. The post cards were marketed for twenty-five cents. For an extra quarter, Noah personalized the signed cards with a drawing of either a Cold River trout or buck.

THE HERMIT OF COLD RIVER

Four months following Paoli Troop 1's visit to the hermitage, the 65-year-old hermit's picture and the story of his long life in the mountains appeared in *The New York State Conservationist*, October-November 1946 issue, written by Clayt Seagears of the widely-read magazine. The story launched the hermit into the limelight of public attention.

Seagears was the first director and writer of the Division of Conservation Education and chief architect in 1946 of its new publication. Al Bromley, a former editor of *The Conservationist* said, "No one who ever heard Clayt talk…ever forgot him." Seagears, known as "Mr. Conservation," was a showman who loved the 1940s–50s New York Sportsmen's Shows. He was admired for his natural history-conservation field of illustrated writings, sketches, drawings, cartoons, oil and watercolors as well as his Conservationist series, "The Inside on the Outdoors."

Seagears described the hieroglyphics Noah used in his secret-coded writing as an "operation very closely resembling the tracks of an inebriated hen whose father was a devilish rooster and whose maternal parent could be termed foot-loose."

His article appears below.

There isn't a more bona fide hermit in the whole United States—including Sharktooth Shoal—than Noah John Rondeau, who has occupied a hole in a woodpile way the hell and gone back in the Adirondack wilderness for 33 years.

Noah John is not only the real McCoy in the hermit department; he looks like hermits are supposed to look. He lives the same way.

He has himself a Sunday suit fabricated out of a couple of deer hides and assembled with bear-tooth toggles. He hunts. He fishes. He traps. He uses the longbow. He keeps a diary in secret code and sets his calendar by the stars. He owns less household equipment than a Tenderfoot Scout would take on an overnight hike, and how he gets through a long, zero Adirondack winter in that layout of his is strictly a lesson in hibernation which any woodchuck would do well to look into.

Noah John is, in truth, spang out of this universe.

On being questioned about the New York City chorus girls and actress Arleen Whelan planting kisses on the hermit's beard, Noah defended himself: "I didn't kiss them. They kissed me. Men and women seem to be doing a lot of screaming about all those young girls that have kissed the hermit. The fact is that the old maids and some other ladies are jealous because they haven't had their kisses yet. The men have their noses out of joint because the Bells won't kiss them. My answer is to the ladies, Seek and ye shall find. To the men, Raise pretty whiskers." From the cover of a sportsmen's show brochure.

Perhaps we shouldn't wait to the breathless finish of this yarn to give out with a rich moral. We have a State with darned near fourteen million people in it [in 1946], the teemingest population in the nation. Yet here's a guy wanting to be a hermit who was able to be one with a minimum of outside interference, and in a peak-studded wilderness six hours by forest foot-trail from the nearest hamlet. The moral thus seems to be that (1) Noah John is one in fourteen million and (2) that despite a population density of 250 folks per square mile we still have large quantities of country for people to lose themselves in when pressed (for various reasons) for a walk in spaces very wide and very wild.

On November 26 and 27, 1930 Oscar Burguiere helped Noah move an anvil from an abandoned Santa Clara lumber camp located high in Ouluska Pass which the hermit called Anvil Camp. Courtesy Richard J. Smith from Rondeau's photo album

Leave us draw up a hunk of balsam stump while Noah John cooks what very well may turn out to be his whole day's "vittles"—a few flapjacks bogged down with his own brand of syrup.

This cooking function is performed (in summer) over a more or less perpetual open fire. He flaps the jacks in bear grease, rolls them up like a cigar, bites off about up to the band and then takes a healthy swig of syrup out of a bottle still ketchupy around the seams. Nuts, says Noah, to the napkin trade.

And let us gaze (withal, with awe) upon the unique living quarters of Noah John. What appear to be wooden tepees in the photo on the next page are indeed wooden tepees—but of a variety more practical than anything ever described in the Manual of Carpentry and Tinkery for Growing Boys. Noah John lives in his own woodpile. Come spring, he has burned his kitchenette, his storage vault, his front parlor and his powder room behind him. Furthermore, he has made it easy to do.

The system is this: When winter has run itself out down the mountain rivers, Noah John starts building his tepee village. He cuts long poles of efficient burning diameter. Every three feet he notches them nearly through. Then he stacks 'em up like a wigwam, leaving an interior recess large enough to stretch out in. Thus, when winter has piled the drifts high and our hermit's activity has been reduced to a minimum, the chore of keeping a fire is a cinch. Noah John merely reaches out the door, removes a pole, gives it a belt with the axe head, and the notched pieces fall apart. He admits it took him a few years to figure out the proper deal for this easy-living angle; but what do a few years amount to in a pattern of life such as his?

Noah John Rondeau, whose nearest neighbor was 19 miles distant, lived in the isolated Cold River region in the very heart of the Adirondacks. His callers were few, he had no radio, he didn't even boast the luxury of a kerosene lamp, and he hadn't even a clock—but withal, he was happy.
Courtesy Richard J. Smith from Rondeau's photo album

Noah John is 63 years old. He now finds it bad news to do his main sleeping under a drafty canopy of slanted poles. So, he has a hovel made from a few boards off a long defunct lumber camp. Over the so-called door to this

Uneducated formally, Noah nevertheless had read of Thoreau and his Walden; of the battle of the ants, of the peace and quiet a philosopher might acquire when separated from civilization.
Courtesy Albert C. "Bud" Smith

Fall 1947. "I spend my Leisure hours Writing and reading Poetry. I suppose if I could write Prose I would be on Easy Street and if I could write Poetry, I would Own the Street. Neither has happened but I like to write anyways."—Noah John Rondeau

Noah's writing casts a long shadow on his past, a shadow where he was most affected by Nature and developed his magical aptitude for observation and his still dimly perceived ability to express himself. History may readily assess the economics and politics that condemned the man to find his liberty in the mountains, but it also conceals from us the student trapped by a lack of education. After all, Rondeau's personal history as we know it is in his written record, in interviews with reporters and in the memories of relatives and friends. Courtesy Dr. Adolph G. Dittmar Jr.

realm of retirement the old boy has nailed a sign "TOWN HALL." Inside there's just room enough for a sort of bed and a crude stove. Every year the place gets smaller, due to encroachment of soot layers from the walls. On the bed is just what you'd expect to find on the bed of a better class hermit—a bear skin. The interior has touches here and there of gaudy décor—the stalagmite drippings of myriad red, yellow and white candles. There are no windows and none are necessary, because the occupant is, perforce, always close to the door. It's as simple as that.

He has another cubbyhole for the convenience of visiting firemen—the hikers who occasionally call on him. This jointed shelter does have a window, and more extensive decoration—the chalky shoulder blades of a dozen beavers, the antlers of bygone bucks and the skulls of two degreased bears. These rattle nicely in the breeze and add to the general cheer.

Noah John, despite his thirty-three long years of complete isolation, and despite the primitive aspects of his existence, is by no means uncouth or illiterate. By any yardstick of human behavior, he is a distinctly bright gent. It would be difficult, in fact, to find a single button missing, except on his pants. He loves to talk—picturesque hermit talk if he thinks his hiker-visitor would be made any happier by it. He reads anything he can lay hands on, but leans to books on astronomy, philosophy, and kindred subjects of the solitudes. This is quite understandable.

By 1946, Noah had lived in the woods thirty-three years off and on—fifteen years straight he worked at being a hermit right on Cold River Bluff. He literally had all the beauty of the Adirondack Mountains in his backyard. Courtesy Edward Blankman (The Lloyd Blankman Collection)

He likes people (if they don't crowd him), but it is suspected that he views them with some suspicion. Inherently honest himself, Noah John hints darkly that it was a sequence of sharp practices by others, when he was the youthful proprietor of a barber chair, which drove him from what he felt was a chiseling world to the honesty of open spaces.

Noah, who confessed to being 63 years old in 1946, stood five feet, five inches tall and weighed 140 pounds. Straight down below his cabin and wigwams, at the foot of a 75-foot drop, winds the Cold River. On the opposite bank rugged Panther Peak rears its 4,000 feet. From the doorstep of the Town Hall, his cabin, Santanoni Mountain and peaks of the Seward Range enhanced a panoramic view, that was a veritable fairyland of charm in his day. Today the bluff is entirely wooded. Author's collection

Noah John's outdoors is built to order for a hermit. His spot is on a bluff high over the end of Cold River Flow, twelve miles as the crow flies south of Lower Saranac Lake, ten miles northeast of Long Lake Village and twenty miles west of Keene Valley. Trails maintained by the Conservation Department lead all the way—about nineteen miles of hiking in any direction, except that eleven miles can be made by canoeing to the north end of Long Lake, thence into the Raquette and then a mile or so up the Cold. Most hikers go in via Long Lake Village and Shattuck Clearing, although some prefer the hoof route via Corey's (just south of Upper Saranac) and Mountain Pond. Four miles to Noah John's east are Preston Ponds, nestling at the end of Indian Pass. He couldn't have picked a more isolated place to live with a Ouija board.

"I do sewing of patches on ten year old underwear."—**N.J. Rondeau.** Courtesy Burton Rondeau

Preparing his much-needed yearly wood supply. Noah constructed two huts for himself, both of which were half underground for natural insulation against the severe Adirondack winters. For heat he used a crude furnace, which was nothing more than an oil drum with its top cut off.

Courtesy Richard J. Smith from Rondeau's photo album

Nor could he have picked a spot of greater beauty. Towering across Noah's valley is Panther Mountain, and Santanoni and Henderson. Behind him rear Seymour, Seward and the Sawtooths. He lives on a strip of [former] lumber company holdings in the middle of a huge chunk of State land comprising about 130 square miles.

Jack Harmes and Noah chat in 1946. Jack said, "Noah was very knowledgeable in identifying wild edible plants. He had time to cultivate flower and vegetable gardens around his hermitage and in other lumber clearings which survived from the days when the area was a thriving logging center. He raised flowers and vegetables which did not appeal to marauding deer. Courtesy Edward R. Harmes

It's wild land, a stronghold of marten and fisher. Noah used to run a 40-mile trap line when he was more spry. Now he has all he can do to "come out" once a year for a packbasket of staples. Forest Rangers—like Orville Betters or Wayne Tyler—or deer hunters and hikers bring him his mail now and then, plus small supplies of food. Or Fred McLane, the Conservation Department's head plane pilot, may drop him bread and papers. Maybe the brook trout are biting in Noah John's Lost Pond or in Cold River Flow. Maybe a snowshoe rabbit rams its head against Noah John's sittin' log and conks out conveniently in time for a lonely, February meal. Maybe.

The Conservation Department has a great friend in Noah John. Spry or not—if anything went wrong in the woods, he'd be out of there on all two cycles to tell the boys about it. He's a great friend of Man in General, too. For

Expert at Woodlore, early 1934. For hunting Noah used both guns and bow-and-arrows. The latter, which he used for smaller game, was homemade, and amazingly accurate. His homemade arrows had steel heads cut from a crosscut saw which had been filed to razor-sharpness. Courtesy Richard J. Smith from Rondeau's photo album

he's the magnet which lures many a hiker deep into some of the grandest country in the world, and that kind of stuff is good for what ails you.

Yep, everything considered, there's quite a guy behind all that alfalfa.

"Noah ran away at the age of 12 and was adopted by a Presbyterian minister in Vermont," recalled Jay Gregory. "Rondeau picked up his courteous manner. He was the most courteous man I ever met—he was almost Chesterfieldian." Author's collection

The helicopter which Noah described as being much like "a little red dragon fly" brought him from his hermitage in Cold River to the outside world. Upon landing in New York City, the bearded hermit was descended on by a bevy of blonde chorus girls who planted kisses on his chin tufts before flashing cameras. "I didn't kiss them," he said. "They kissed me." Courtesy New York State Museum

On Tuesday, January 6, 1948, at Saranac Lake from 7 to 9 P.M. Noah posed for sketches under the direction of artist William Rowe at Hotel Alpine Studio. Courtesy Douglas Nessle

OPPOSITE BOTTOM: A typical hermit autograph. Courtesy Douglas Nessle

Noah welcomed visitors to his replica hermitage display. He would state of his secluded existence that he simply loved the woods. Richard J. Smith from Rondeau's photo album

Noah signed hundreds of autographs on the backs of 8x10 glossy photographs and personalized postcards he had ordered and sold for fifty cents. Richard J. Smith from Rondeau's photo album

Noah enjoyed sharing his life's story, stating that he had followed the barber trade in Lake Placid, Bloomingdale and also in Saranac Lake. He spoke of the old Jerry Pasho barber shop where he had worked for some time. It was the love of the woods that brought him to the mountain fastness at Cold River, and he said he was perfectly satisfied with his life there. Courtesy Richard J. Smith from Rondeau's photo album

During Noah's February 1947 time in New York City, he hobnobbed with the famous actress Arlene Whelan, who took him on a tour of Paramount Studios. Courtesy Richard J. Smith from Rondeau's photo album

One of a number of glossy 8x10 photos Noah marketed. On January 20, 1949 Noah ordered 1,000 photographs from Acosta Studio in Saranac Lake, N.Y. He had accepted a contract from Campbell-Fairbanks to attend the Boston Sportsmen's Show and wanted to be prepared. Studio Photo

SOME HERMIT REMEMBRANCES OF FRIENDS, ACQUAINTANCES, AND ONE JOHNNY-COME-LATELY

"**E**J. Dailey possessed a vast knowledge of wildlife amassed over seventy years of trapping. He lived in a forsaken cabin of the Santa Clara Lumber Company on Cold River and trapped fisher and marten over the contiguous Santanoni, Seward, Saw Tooth, and Ampersand Mountains deep in the Adirondack wilderness. His only neighbor was Noah Rondeau."—*Donald Jack Anderson, outdoors writer*

Noah, circa early 1930s.

"Rondeau He scraped like a madman on a broken fiddle and once killed a bear with a homemade longbow and sometimes fired any weapon that was handy at the folks who approached the place."—*E.J. Dailey, fellow trapper and outdoors writer*

"I used to fish the Black Hole area of the Cold River in the early days. Rondeau lived in some huts down river. His presence was a sore spot with some of the local game protectors. Earl Vosburgh was the main source of trouble. Rondeau claimed the protectors planted illegally obtained meat and furs at his camp. He was eventually vindicated on all charges but he lost his guide's license any ways. That is why Rondeau carved "EARL VOSBURGH IS AN ALL--AMERICAN SON-OF-A-BITCH" on a big pine log that laid across an old lumber road that went up alongside of Boulder Brook.

"One time, when guiding a party in the Cold River country, I stopped by Rondeau's. He was sitting in his rocker looking over the Cold River and admiring the view of Santanoni. He liked to hear the news about Tupper and things that were going on. Before leaving he kiddingly quizzed my party of fishermen as to whether they would want to buy a mountain." *Fredric C. Reeves, Tupper Lake guide*

Noah referred to conversations with visitors as "confab sessions."

"Although Noah ridiculed anyone who smoked for breathing smoke instead of clean Adirondack air, it was Uncle Roy who got Noah to smoke a pipe and drink whiskey. That was after 1925 when Noah started visiting Roy and his family, who settled near Bartlett Carry."—*Carl Hathaway*

"The year was 1935. I was camping and trapping in the 'Dacks in the woods above Shattuck Clearing. A man peeked at me from behind a clump of trees; before I knew it I could feel some sort of power or uneasiness. I stopped my activities several times to look around but never saw anyone. When a tattle-tale blue jay began to scold I became more alert and eventually eyed someone spying on me. I was real careful; I'd come onto a man's still in the woods once. I looked right at the figure and said friendly like, "Howdy" but the person didn't come right out with the usual "Hi" that I had expected. Finally he stepped out. I waved a salute and he replied. He invited me to his camp—his 'city' as he spoke of it. It was very unusual and I couldn't get over his wigwam method of drying firewood."—*Don Bowman, trapper and author of several local history books*

"We had descended Couchi [hikers' nickname for Couchsachraga Mountain] maybe later than we should have but felt we had sufficient time to reach the hermit's before nightfall. He was expecting us. Unfortunately, sundown came as we were in the middle of Belly Ache swamp, Noah's name for the swamp across the river from his hermitage. We became disoriented. I was never so happy as when we eyed the light from his kerosene lantern and heard him call. We were rescued from what could have been an uncomfortable night spent in a swamp."—*Charlotte Dittmar Murray, mountain climber*

"Noah was a most agreeable host; he treated my party well when we fished the Cold River in the 1930s. He never failed to fix up his guest tent or wigwam with fresh grass for matting and even had a centerpiece of wild flowers placed in a jar on a shelf to welcome us each spring. I never had any hesitation eating his Everlasting Stew that continually simmered in his iron kettle."—*Vincent Engels, author of* Adirondack Fishing in the 1930s: A Lost Paradise

"My grandfather and dad were forest rangers at Shattuck Clearing; they invited Rondeau into camp and became fast friends."—*Earle Russell*

"My wife's father knew Rondeau. That's how Mary got to know him. Mary and I spent part of our honeymoon at the hermitage in 1943. We went back many times to see our old friend."—*Dr. Adolph "Ditt" Dittmar*

Mary C. Dittmar at "Boiling Pond," during Adolph's and her honeymoon vacation, Sept. 1943.

"My father knew Noah John in the 1920s, that's how I got to know him. I introduced 'Ditt' to Noah about 1939. My sisters and I climbed to the surrounding summits from his Cold River bluff cabins."—*Mary Colyer Dittmar*

"We stayed the night in Noah John's 'guest tent' with bear rugs. Noah John didn't think that three girls should go up Coochie alone. He rowed us across the river and walked a ways to show us where he had hidden bottles of sugar in case he had to sleep out while on his trap line. He ended up on Couchsachraga Peak with us."—*Helen Colyer Menz*

Foreground: Helen Colyer (Menz). Left to Right: Mary Colyer (Dittmar), "Ruthie" Prince, and Noah. Couchsachraga Peak, 1942. Noah joked the "four in the picture were not escaped Russian refugees. The way they got to the Mountain Top was eating Bread and Candy and drinking Lemonade...."

Maude Gregory never passed up a cup of Noah's rich brewed coffee.

"When my backpacking party arrived at the hermitage Noah was there with two doctors, annual visitors during fishing season. He fixed his famous coffee for us. The coffee was so thick you'd swear it could hold a spoon in an upright position!"—*Ruth Coyler King*

"Noah first met my first husband, Phil McCalvin, when he served in the Civilian Conservation Corps side camp near Mountain Pond. They became close friends. Noah used our couch as a bed, often for months at a time. We enjoyed having him stay with us. He was like another member of the family."—*Helen Sawatzki*

Gary McCalvin and Noah.

"From the mid-1940s on Noah would frequently visit my brother's and my lodge—Plumley's Point House—on Long Lake. He liked to sit in one of the Adirondack-style chairs on our dock and wave to our guests as they got off the launch."—*Jim Plumley, co-owner of Plumly's Point Lodge*

"My father was a forest ranger. He used to accompany Noah to sportsmen's shows, being responsible for arranging the lodging, handling the money, being a companion and such. Seeing the hermit and listening to him address my school class was a special experience that created a lasting impression."—*John Longware, Forest Ranger*

"Noey used to be my father's fishing guide in the 1920's. Dad once put-up bail money and supported the hermit at his trial."—*Peggy Byrne, writer*

"Noah's long-time friend Bill Petty and I attended his burial. Bill placed a granite rock on top of his grave, saying he thought that rock just might keep the hermit down."—*Wayne Byrne, Plattsburgh businessman and outdoorsman*

"My husband, Ed, and I went to Plumley's Point House, by boat. It was at the far [north] end of Long Lake. From there we would hike to Shattuck Clearing, and then follow the Cold River right up to the Hermitage. We only took day trips when we visited Noah John, toting gifts and me carrying a decorated birthday cake in my hand the entire fourteen miles. The only time I ever carried anything in my hands while hiking."—*Grace Hudowalski, first woman to climb all forty-six highest Adirondack peaks*

Jim Plumley's dock, on Long Lake, was a popular hangout for Noah throughout the 1940s.

"Noah was my father's unofficial caretaker and guardian of Camp Seward, a small green-timber cabin father and Jay Gregory had for hunting and fishing tucked secretively into the wilderness down river from Noah's."—*C.V. Latimer Jr., M.D.*

Noah labeled this: "A Best Old Lover."

"I used to drive Noah out to the highway (Route 3). He'd wait for me in our kitchen—told my wife he enjoyed her Christmas cookies."—*Lucien Martin, caretaker for Avery Rockefeller's Ampersand Park*

"In 1920 my father and Noah worked together for a short time. It was a temporary job in the Saranac Lake vicinity. Mr. Rondeau was a familiar figure in Lewis [near Elizabethtown in Essex County] every Christmas as he spent that holiday there with friends. I reestablished ties with him in 1943 when he came to address my junior high school assembly."—*Marilyn Hathaway Cross, author of* Growing Up Strong

"My dad first met Noah in the 1930s when climbing in the Seward Mountains and Couchsachraga Peak. When I was a teenager the hermit guided me on random scoots over abandoned logging roads and deer trails in order that I could reach the tops of the last of my forty-six peaks."—*John M. Harmes, lawyer*

Richard J. Smith, Summer 1934.

"Noah called me son; I liked that. He was father-like to me. We were good friends. We shared a great many enjoyable years together in camp, fishing, hunting, trapping, plus a great many random scoots along old trails through the wonderful Cold River Valley.

"Noah was never bigger-than-life although some people portrayed him that way in print. He wouldn't have liked that image. He was a commoner and right proud of himself just the way he was."—*Richard "Red" Smith, Great Camp caretaker*

"I believe Noah was always on the lookout for more food and I know that my Albany Chapter of ADK [the Adirondack Mountain Club] led frequent trips to his camp. We always left food with him in appreciation for his guiding services and use of his camp."—*Bill White, frequent visitor to the hermitage*

"I was told to level the hermit's cabins with the bulldozer following the end of the Oval Wood Dish Corporation' s culling logging operation following the 1950 'Big Blow.' I sat on that caterpillar, my hand on the levers facing the Town Hall, but I could not bring myself to destroy the simple shelter that Noah had lived in for thirty-five years. I've heard outsiders say Adirondack natives don't have much appreciation for their own history. I know better. I was determined that at least one of Rondeau's huts and his belongings be preserved for its history."—*Harvey Carr, logger and an original member of the Liar's Club*

"Harvey Carr took my husband and me to Cold River bluff to see Rondeau's structures. We felt there was so much local history in those buildings. Along with other interested people we convinced Bruce Inverarity (first director of the Adirondack Museum) that the Cold River hermit's cabins would make a very popular display. By himself, Harvey dismantled, hauled out and re-assembled Rondeau's Town Hall."—*Eleanor Webb, co-owner of Hemlock Hall, Blue Mountain Lake*

"I've admired Noah ever since I shook hands with him in New York City when the Conservation Department had a setup in the sportsmen's show in 1947. He was kind to me; I was seventeen years old then."—*Stephen Klein Jr., ardent hiker and Long Lake camp owner*

"As a child, then teenager and finally young adult, I believed writing to and receiving mail and pictures from a real hermit was neat."—*Bonnie Warner, Adirondack native*

"When I saw Noah at the New York City sportsmen's show I was struck by the tragedy of his 'discovery.' I felt sorrow for him for I received the distinct impression that he had lost control of his life and if he ever returned to Cold River he would never regain the beauty of what he had experienced."—*Richard Benson, business owner*

"I was a KSLU student radio reporter for St. Lawrence University. I interviewed Rondeau at the ranger station in Saranac Lake. The hermit spent quite a lot of time reciting poetry he had composed back in the woods."—*Leslie Farmer, interview by the author*

"I was a radio announcer at ABC in New York City assigned to cover the sportsmen's show. I invited Noah to come to the studio one evening. It was my job to find interesting spots for the late evening sports program. Eyeing the hermit with his beard and hearing his sharp native sense of humor I thought he would be perfect—just what I was looking for. Following the interview, I asked him to accompany me to Hurley's Bar, where we continued to visit."—*Dorian St. George, radio personality*

"For several years, I had a canvas wall tent set up down river, in the vicinity of High Banks, from Rondeau's. Noah often joined my deer hunting party—driving Holy Lost, Dismal and other swamps he knew so well. I have an 8mm home movie of him taking a ride over the snow atop a large buck we killed"—*Clarence E. Whiteman, avid white-tail deer hunter*

"I worked for the Lake Placid Flying Club. In my spare time I would air drop canned goods to the 'mayor'. He'd show his appreciation for each delivery by dancing a jig as he wove around his tiny cabin."—*Charlie W. Smith, pilot*

"As my hiking party ate lunch with Rondeau, a boy's camp counselor tuned the hermit's fiddle. It was terribly out of tune. I take it the old fella didn't like the sound of the instrument afterwards because he promptly retuned it to his liking!"

Noah presents a hand-picked flower from his garden to an Adirondack Mountain Club hiker.

"I was co-chairman of the Burnt Hills Sportsmen's Show sponsored by the Explorer Scout Post 38, Schenectady Council. Noah John stayed at my home for two nights. We enjoyed his visit; he was quite talkative and friendly—not my idea of a hermit. The show was a huge success in part because of his attendance.

"When I heard Noah was in town for a sportsmen's show I asked him to come around to the hospital to see the boys ward; I figured they would be thrilled to see a genuine hermit. Noah didn't let me down. At the appointed time I picked him up. He was decked out in furs and had all sorts of woods trinkets. For all the world he looked the part of a hermit. What excitement! Noah told the children about Cold River and his life in the woods—he probably embellished it a bit as he passed around his furs, articles of clothing, and such. The next week I showed up at the hospital to find that all the kids who had met Noah had broken out in a mysterious skin irritation; the boys had had to have their heads shaven and the ward was quarantined."—*Edward Miller, scout master and businessman*

"When we finally arrived at Rondeau's mountain retreat, we got a big surprise. The old fellow came out, said 'Hello gentlemen,' and then handed us his Cold River metropolis guest register which we were asked to sign. We wondered whether we'd heard correctly, and inquired, 'We thought you were a hermit?' to which Rondeau retorted, 'I am, but what's the use of being a hermit if you don't meet a lot of people?'"—*Charles Mooney, City Editor of the* Knickerbocker News

"Noey would board a bus that stopped near his place, Singing Pines, in Wilmington and come over to my home several times each week. I can still see him stepping off the Greyhound, walking up the drive and entering my home. The door was always open for him. He'd plunk himself down in the kitchen rocker next to the wood-fired kitchen range and just sit quietly smoking and rocking for hours."—*Madeline Dodge, Au Sable Forks school librarian*

"Some kids would bring their pets to school, others would share experiences about places they visited. I brought Noah John Rondeau to share with my fifth-grade class in Tupper Lake."—*Carl Hathaway, Adirondack boat builder*

"I interviewed Rondeau back in the 1930's and '40s and ran some stories on his doings years before he became the darling of the Conservation Department and the star player in sportsmen's shows. I recall being decidedly unimpressed with his housekeeping."—*Louis Simmons, Tupper Lake historian, author and newspaper editor*

Bette O'Hern stands at the site of Rondeau's Cold River hermitage, 2007. The memorial plaque, that marked the spot for fifteen years has since been taken by an assumed trophy-seeker.

"Noah lived for a while with Harley and Sally Branches on the old Lake Colby Drive. I remember passing him when I drove the school bus. In cold weather he always wore a heavy black coat that went almost down to his knees. It had a sort of stand-up collar and big buttons on the front. His hat wasn't the typical style of the day either. You'd notice him right away because he was dressed differently."—*Theodore Hillman, proprietor of Stoneyland Cottages*

"I recall being at Mrs. Brad's home one day during the winter when Noah stopped by. He mentioned he thought he was coming down with a cold. Mrs. B thinking the old gentleman could use some vitamin C, offered Noah a lemon. Instead of taking it home he surprised both of us. He took out his pocketknife and sliced the lemon in half. Then he squeezed each half with one fist, catching the juice in his opposite cupped hand. Then he did the most outlandish thing; With great suction he sniffed the juice right up into his nose. We were both very surprised. I suppose it was just another one of his folksy home remedies. And who knows. Maybe it did some good.

"Another time, in the 1950s, when I worked at Montgomery Ward's in Saranac Lake, one of my co-workers, Helen Mc Calvin, came to work fairly disgusted one day. At that time Noah was living at her house. Her husband, Phil, and Noah were old friends. It seems Noah was in charge of her little boy when she worked. He was a good sitter but on this one occasion when she returned home she was astonished to see Noah spooning dog food out of a can and feeding it to her son."—*Mrs. Theodore Hillman*

"One afternoon in late July 1992 I began seriously working on cracking Rondeau's code. Once I identified all the characters it was just a matter of figuring out which symbols stood for which letters. Or, so I thought! Unfortunately, there (were no) most commonly used symbols no matter how big a sample I took—it was a close race between about five different characters. That tended to indicate that either the code wasn't a letter-substitution cipher, or it wasn't in English or French. Both possibilities seemed unlikely; there was something else, I decided, mixing up the count. So, I threw the statistical analysis out the window and after a day and a half went hunting for patterns. There I struck pay dirt."—*David Greene, discovered the key for deciphering Noah's secret code*

A LOOK BACK IN TIME
Adirondack Logger Rescues an Iconic Hermit's Cabin

Logger Harvey Carr thought to save Adirondack
hermit Noah John Rondeau's cabin from the bulldozer

Life went on for the Paoli scouts of Troop 1. As members pursued degrees, began careers, and started families, Noah John Rondeau's life also evolved.

Four years following the scouts' visit the Cold River hermit permanently moved from his picturesque woodland haunt for the tame comforts of Wilmington, N.Y.

Noah's thirty-three-year sojourn there had given the spot its own peculiar atmosphere—smelly, perhaps, but still the favorite destination of people from many places. For years, hikers and fishermen had made their way in to Cold River via Shattuck's and the fishing, good as it was, was invariably incidental to a visit with the hirsute old character. His explanation was simply this: "I left because I am wearing out."

Bill White stands next to Rondeau's Town Hall hut. By 1967, the structure was in a weakened state of decay. Courtesy Bill White

Over the years souvenir hunters picked through the hermitage. This collector carried the Town Hall door to his boat docked at Plumley's Point on Long Lake. Author's collection

I would venture a guess that if the former scouts had learned the very disturbing rumor making the rounds of the Cold River country that the lumbering outfit making rapid inroads into the hardwood growth of the area had decided to bulldoze the huts and tepees down the embankment, they would not have been the only persons who would be alarmed to think that such a thing might happen to the grassy knoll.

This is the story of how one man thought Rondeau's habitation should be left intact because it epitomized a type of existence led by many others before Noah's hegira to the wilderness. All traces of the other hermits have long since faded away. Why should not this one be allowed to stand as long as nature permits? It is too much of an attraction to be obliterated and its passing would be lamented by many.

Noah John Rondeau was a hermit who lived alone in the woods of the Cold River basin in New York's Adirondack Mountains. There he built his own hermitage and lived for 30 years in two small cabins and some wigwams. He had decided to become a hermit, he said, to escape "the slavery of industrialism." After a windstorm wrecked his camp in 1950, Rondeau moved out of the woods and spent the last 17 years of his life living as a boarder.

When the abandoned residence was about to be bulldozed in 1959 to complete a contract cutting, local logger Harvey Carr thought it was a shame that this piece of Rondeau's life would be destroyed. With some help from Eleanor and Monty Webb, owners of The Cliff Hanger Resort in Blue Mountain Lake, along with renewed interest in the hermit's life from the media, the curator

Logger Harvey Carr, foreground, spearheaded the project to save Noah John Rondeau's Cold River residence from the bulldozer.

of the Adirondack Museum [now known as The Adirondack Experience], Dr. Bruce Inverarity, became convinced that a remaining cabin was worth saving. He granted Carr permission to transport it to the museum's grounds.

The cabin was made of notched hemlock logs with a bark-covered roof and had a built-in log bunk and stove.

Mary Carr ponders the isolation of the hermit's huts before the removal operation. The Hall of Records is in the foreground. The Town Hall is in the background. This once open setting is entirely wooded today.

As Eleanor Webb recalls, as soon as permission from Inverarity was granted, Carr took on the arduous job of moving the cabin to the museum. "He painstakingly numbered each log, each board, and each item, carefully dismantled it all, and prepared it for travel the long way out over the rough logging road. He was almost defeated trying to get some help and some way of transportation out [to the museum]. I think one man [Paul Crofut] helped him after he had gotten the consent of the museum to send a truck. Then Harvey put it all carefully together again on the farthest-out perimeter of the grounds." Later on, the cabin was moved to an indoor exhibit.

In March of 1991, Harvey Carr told me about how Rondeau's cabin was brought out of the woods and became part of the Adirondack Museum's collection:

We [the logging crew] went into Cold River in the fall of 1958. I was working for Paul Crofut, the logging contractor, who was working for the Northern Lumber Company. The US Bobbin and Shuttle Company owned the property—they're the company that made wooden spools and such.

We stayed in there during the winter at the lumber camp. We cut the hardwood and brought it out and sometime during the late winter or going toward spring, somebody from the US Shuttle and Bobbin Company came into camp and told us, before we got down toward Rondeau's camp, they wanted us to take the dozer down, smash it up, bury it and get rid of all the lumber and everything because they were afraid of hunters moving in and causing a forest fire. Of course, that wasn't a bad idea, but you know, there was brush and weeds and a lot of slash… Anyway, they wanted us to destroy it completely.

Paul Crofut and Harvey Carr loading salvaged timber near Cold River.

I sat there in the logging camp that night and said to the boys, 'I hate to see it go…Gee, it's too bad. It should be in a museum or something.' Then I hadn't even thought about it for two, three, four days and then I got to talking about it again. You know, like it would be a shame to tear it all apart, bury it and everything. And about then, Jack Swancott, one of the truck drivers, gave me the idea. Real casual like he says, 'Well you got a museum right there in Blue Mountain Lake.'

I said, 'Oh yeah, but I don't know if they'd be at all interested or not. Naw, I doubt they'd want it.'

Jacky said, 'Well maybe they would.'

'Course we stayed in there [at the lumber camp] all week and it would come and go on my mind. So...I stopped up there [at the museum]. Oh, it was late January or February '59.

Left to right: Eleanor Webb, Monty Webb, Mary Carr inside the cabin.

I mentioned how I felt to Monty and Eleanor [Webb]. They liked that sort of thing—old stuff, antiques and all. I also went up there [to the museum] and stopped to talk to Ralph Raymond. Ralph was the custodian up there. He lives up there year-round and takes care of the place. I explained all about Rondeau's camp and so forth but he didn't get too enthused about it. He didn't know much about it, but I remember Ralph saying to me, 'You ought to talk to Dr. Inverarity.'

Sometime soon afterward I told Eleanor and Monty about the old hermit camp, and later I took them into Cold River. We drove up in my truck. We stopped at the lumber camp, ate lunch…[and talked about Rondeau]. Monty said they'd talk to Dr. Inverarity. It wasn't long after Monty, Eleanor, Mary [Carr's wife] and I had returned home from Cold River that we were sitting eating supper, and right along I got a telephone call from the operator saying this was a person-to-person call from Dr. Inverarity in New York City. He had heard from Ralph and the Webbs. He said, 'I hear there is a possibility that we could get Noah John Rondeau's camp. By all means, we'd like it if you can get it out.'

He even talked of sending a helicopter crew up there with some carpenters who could build a framework around it and airlift it from there to the museum. Knowing the camp's condition and the woods and so on, I knew what I wanted to do. You know they were even going to send a television crew and all that stuff and it was going to be getting late [in the season]…

I didn't think Rondeau would care too much about that idea. Of course, he had no legal hold on anything back there anyway, but morally it was still his camp. I told Inverarity that if he wants it, we'll bring it out. 'What I'll do is take it apart piece by piece. I'll number every part and put it back together exactly the way it was and it will be about the same camp.'

I know when I mentioned it to Dr. Inverarity, he sounded excited, just like a kid after you offer 'em some candy. He was tickled to death.

I'd been a lumberjack, not a carpenter, but I knew I was going to do it my way. So, I brought it out, all by myself along with an old iron stove, some cookin' kettles, a coffee pot, as well as a hollow stump Rondeau had used as a 'wet sink' and the only thing I replaced were the bottom logs.

Of course, it's all inside [now] under temperature control, and it's good I suppose for at least for 150 years.

The original museum display was outside.

As for Rondeau, nothing ever pleased him as completely or humbled him as sincerely as being honored by the Adirondack Museum's Cold River hermit exhibit. That seems clear in this letter to Dr. C.V. Latimer Sr.:

> "Yes, my Cold River City, is a shrine at Adirondack Museum at Blue Mountain and I am more proud of it than I would be of all the shrines of Traitorous H.S.T. [President Harry S. Truman] and Dexter White on top of it."

Now, more than half a century after logger Carr's effort to preserve what he felt needed protecting, Rondeau's exhibit has continued to intrigue museum visitors. Thanks to an Adirondack logger, people can still learn about the Adirondack hermit.

Acknowledgements and Dick Henderson's Reflection | William J. O'Hern

My sincere appreciation goes to Dick Henderson. If he had never read *Noah John Rondeau's Adirondack Wilderness Days* (The Forager Press, 2009), and not inquired if I knew anything about Rondeau's Sunday, June 23, 1946 diary entry that read: "16 men and boys come, go (Penn. Scouts)" this book never would have been written.

I would also like to acknowledge Neal Burdick, my editor, for suggestions in the planning and final preparation of the book. Special thanks to the entire group Dick Henderson tapped, to them I am indebted. I am grateful to Nancy Did It! for a superb cover design, restoration of the old photographs, and layout that added new life, beauty, and meaning to *A Classic Adirondack Paddle*.

☆ ☆ ☆

Months after the "Paddle" manuscript had been proofread, Dick continued to reflect on the scout's expedition and his Adirondack years following his troop's classic paddle.

He wrote: "The question came up as to how those Paoli 1 scouts on that very long day of their visit to Cold River City were able to do a lot of those things that must be done, plus those things that were done just for the fun of it. The answer that comes to mind is the energy of youth.

Dick Henderson dreams of a long-ago paddle.

"The last days of the Summer Season of 1948 at Johns Brook Lodge, above Keene Valley in the Adirondacks, were quite indeed. The lodge was preparing for the coming winter, while some degree of resting and hiking continued. On the morning of the very last day we, with bulging packs on our backs, headed down the long trail to the Garden, and then, car-on-road, made the final decent into Keene Valley. After stowing our packs, the climb to the summit of Giant Mountain allowed us to pensively eat lunch while gazing at expansive silver Lake Champlain, with Mount Mansfield looming in Vermont, and the Cloud-Splitter behind us. And then down, down, down, running, laughing, laughing and shouting, down Giant Mountain to the road and the bus station and home."

Index